SAVING OUR WORLD HERITAGE

LEO HOPKINSON

Published by the United Nations Educational, Scientific and Cultural Organization (UNESCO), 7, place de Fontenoy, 75352 Paris 07 SP, France, and The Watts Publishing Group Limited (on behalf of its publishing imprint Franklin Watts, a division of Hachette Children's Group), Carmelite House, 50 Victoria Embankment, London EC4Y 0DZ, United Kingdom.

© UNESCO and The Watts Publishing Group Limited (on behalf of its publishing imprint Franklin Watts, a division of Hachette Children's Group), 2022

UNESCO's ISBN: 978-92-3-100508-4 (hardback)
978-92-3-100498-8 (paperback)
Franklin Watts' ISBN: 978 1 4451 6743 5 (hardback)
978 1 4451 6744 2 (paperback)

One year following first publication of this book, electronic files of the content will be available under the terms of a CC-BY-NC-ND 3.0 IGO license whereby use and re-distribution of the Work are allowed on the basis that there is a superimposed watermark across each page to say 'Not for commercial use', the original source is properly quoted and each recipient may use the Work only under the terms of the CC-BY-NC-ND 3.0 IGO license. Commercial re-distribution and derivative works are not allowed under this license without prior authorization from UNESCO and the Watts Publishing Group Limited. By using the content of this publication, the users accept to be bound by the terms of use of the UNESCO Open Access Repository (www.unesco.org/open-access/terms-use-ccbyncnd-en).

The designations employed and the presentation of material throughout this publication do not imply the expression of any opinion whatsoever on the part of UNESCO concerning the legal status of any country, territory, city or area or of its authorities, or concerning the delimitation of its frontiers or boundaries.

The ideas and opinions expressed in this publication are those of the authors; they are not necessarily those of UNESCO and do not commit the Organization.

Editorial and picture research: Rachel Cooke and Andrew Cornwell
Design and illustration: Tanya Cooper

Printed and bound in Dubai

Franklin Watts is a Hachette UK company
www.hachette.co.uk
www.franklinwatts.co.uk

Picture credits:

Cover images
Alamy: John Kellerman front cover brar.
iStock: JordiStock back cover c.
Shutterstock: Paola Bona front cover tlb; fizzles front cover trb; Giannakis Photo front cover bla, back cover tlb; Lev Kropotov front cover cl, back cover tl; Leandromery front cover clc; Jacob Lund front cover br, back cover br; Anna Om back cover cl; Omiksovsky front cover bral; PNIKOL front cover bl; Daniel Prudek back cover tbg; Matyas Rehak back cover tc; Roman Sigaev front cover tr; Andriana Suluguic front cover tc; Syda productions front cover tab.
© UNESCO/Asmara Heritage Project, Dr. Edward Edison back cover cr; © UNESCO/Bagayoko Modibo front cover tlc; © UNESCO/Nenadovic front cover tl; © UNESCO/Kishore Rao back cover tcbg.

Interior images
Alamy: Rodolfo Contreras 41tl; Eye Ubiquitous 57t; Greatstock 58cr; Jeffrey Isaac Greenberg 23tr; D Hurst 34; John Kellerman 33cr; David Lyons 9bl; Prisma by Dukas Presseagentur GmbH 15tc, 59tr; Tony Taylor 59tl; Westend61 Gmb 48cr.
Getty Images: Bettmann 39b; Matt Cardy 35bc; DEA/JACCOD/De Agostini 54t; Martin Foster/Nur Photo 11t; Kyodo News 40c, 51b; Giorgio Lotti/Mondadori 41c.
heumarkt-neu.at: 21t.
iStock: JordiStock 16cl; urbancow 15cl.
Parks Canada: Jordan Odney 15tr; Haida Gwaii Watchmen 17c.
Shutterstock: Adwo 15b; Alisa24 18br; mohammad alzain 46c; Antoinee 48-49, 48bl; Uwe Aranas 37t; Artiste2d3d 22-23b; Austinding 40cb; Noel V Baebler 32bl, 33cb; Szymon Bartosz 29bc; A G Baxter 35br; Bayusimpson 36c; Henk Bogaard 19bl; Paolo Bona 14b; Radek Borovka 9cr; Marc Bruxelle 40bc; Eric Buemeye 27br; Pete Burana 18bl; Canadastock 10tr; Rich Carey 26br; Maizai Chaniago 11cr; Dmitry Chulov 9br; Tanjala Cica 56cl; Ivan Soto Cobos 56cr; Corentinmace 41bc; Kobby Dagan 59br; Thomas Dutour 56br; EB Adventure Photography 55c; William Edge 22-23b, 27bcb; Eventh 12-13; fizkes 6b; Nick Fox 32c; Al geba 35t; Giannakis Photo 27c; Gorodenkoff 14cr; Vadim Gouida 8cl; Grandbrothers 47br; Peter Gudella 36cb; Anton Gvozdikov 56bl; Sven Hansche 20br; Igor Hotinsky 47bl; Sean Hsu 18-19 main; HQuality 19br; Ingehogenbijl 37cl; Eric Iselee 48br, 49tl; Anton Ivanov 44-45; Debra James 43b; Ryan Janssens 42tr; Tinnakom jorruang 16bl; michael jung 12b; Kalvic 30-31; Alexsey Kartsev 43tr; Rafael Dias Katayama 55b; Kawing921 6tr; Stephan Kerkhofs 42bl; Kertu 29t; Oleksandr Kotenko 29cb; Jess Kraft 8br; Lev Kropotov 48bc, 55cb; Dimitry Kuznetsov 17bc; Johan Larson 42c; Victor Lauer 55t; Leandromery 27t; Irina Lepneva 23tl; Felix Lipov 21cl; Littlesam 26b; Lorcel 8cr; Lost Mountain Studio 59c; Maridav 8bc; MAR Photography 59bl; Benny Marty 29c,46t; Masx4e 58bc; Mazur Travel 50c; A McIntyre 21blb; MDay Photography 40bc; Meec 32cb; Mehmetcan 44tc; Gena Melendrez 56t; Michelmond 46br; Rudra Narayan Mitra 57c; MN Studio 37bc; Monkey Business Images 17cr; Morenovel 37cr; Nagel Photography 8t, 28cr; NakoPhotography 52c; Paul Nash 20br bg; NDAB Creativity 7br; Kylie Nicholson 26cr; R M Nunes 22t; Nuruddean 20t, 32t, 42tc, 50t; Anna Om 20bl, 22cl; Omiksovsky 36cl; Chansom Pantip 36b, 54b; Pedarilhosbr 27bca; Mike Pellinni 22-23ca; Jamen Percy 41bl; PhotocechCZ 49c; Photographers eu 46bl, 46bc; Photomarine 26t; Photosmatic 33t; PMN Photo 30c; PNIKOL 4; Sergei Primakov 24bl; Daniel Prudek 4bg, 5; Torsten Pursche 51tl; Dan Race 9tl; Rawpixel 7bl, 7bc, 16bcl; Matyas Rehak 35c; Riekephotos 23br; RossHelen 21bla; Saiko3p 52-53; savva_25 24bc; S-F 9c; Graeme Shannon 49bl; Roman Sigaev 41tr; SL-Photography 28cl; Som340 Studio Images 13b; LM Spencer 10b, 15tl; spyarm 38-39; Studio Romantic 36bc, 56cb; Adriana Suluguic 20bc; Sumikophoto 8bl; Sunti 44tr; Syda Productions 16bc,17bl; Linda Szeto 17tl; Tana888 22bl; Sean Thomforde 40br; Tong_stocker 47bc; Alan Tunnicliffe 20c; Twinsterphoto 31c, 33cl; UKRAINE 28br; Sergey Uryadnikov 48cl, 49tr, 49bc; VGstockstudio 32blc; Vladiczech 40bl; Wavebreakmedia 14cl; Richard Whitcombe 54c; Wildestanimal 28cl; Windofchange64 24-25 main; WitR 46cl; Wolfilser 28bc, 29b; Xolodan 15cr; Yvon52 21cr; Konstantin Zadavin 58bl; Sergiy Zavgorodny 42cl.
UNESCO: © UNESCO: 46-47b; © Maamoun Abdulkarim 47c; © UNESCO/AFI-Venise 7t; © UNESCO/Asmara Heritage Project, Dr. Edward Edison 16cr; © UNESCO/Francesco Bandarin 11cl, 47cl, 47b, 50-51b; © UNESCO/Véronique Dauge 46cr, 46b; UNESCO Africa © CRAterre/Sébastien Moriset 17cl, 17cr; © UNESCO/Babayoko Modino 51tr; © UNESCO/Nenadovic 6t; © UNESCO/Ron van Oers 47tr; © UNESCO/Kishore Rao 10tl; © OUR PLACE The World Heritage Collection 9tr, 36cr.

a=above b=below; c=centre; l=left; r=right; t=top; bg= background; tl=top left; tc= top centre; tr= top right; cl=centre left; cr=centre right; bl= bottom left; bc=bottom centre; br= bottom right

Every effort has been made to clear copyright. Should there be any inadvertent omission, please apply to the publisher for rectification.

CONTENTS

	Chapter 1: **Our World Heritage**	4
	How It All Began	6
	The First World Heritage Sites	8
	On the Danger List	10
	Chapter 2: **Heritage in Action**	12
	Meet the Heritage Workers	14
	Involving the Community	16
	Chapter 3: **Expanding Cities**	18
	Building Up Threats	20
	Spreading Outwards	22
	Chapter 4: **Business or Beauty?**	24
	Fishing and Farming	26
	Mining and Logging	28
	Chapter 5: **Here Come the Tourists**	30
	Europe's Historic Cities	32
	Monuments Under Pressure	34
	Nature Under Pressure	36
	Chapter 6: **In Times of Crisis: Disasters**	38
	Fires, Floods and Earthquakes	40
	A Changing Climate	42
	Chapter 7: **In Times of Crisis: Human Conflict**	44
	Conflict In Syria	46
	Conflict In the Rainforests	48
	Rebuilding After War	50
	Chapter 8: **Looking to the Future**	52
	Success Stories	54
	Cultural Journeys	56
	Heritage Evolution	58
	Glossary	60
	Index	62
	Index Of World Heritage Sites	63
	Further Information	64

CHAPTER 1:
OUR WORLD

People today have inherited many things from the past. Some of these things are from nature, while others were made by people. We call this inheritance our world heritage. It includes beautiful landscapes, spectacular buildings, historic cities and ancient monuments. This heritage is something to be valued and protected so that it can be handed on to future generations. This book explores how people work together to save our world heritage.

In many countries, different organisations work to protect our heritage. They may be governments, charities or private companies. However, UNESCO (the United Nations Educational, Scientific and Cultural Organisation) supports these efforts. The United Nations (UN) was set up after the Second World War (1939–1945) to enable the different countries to work together for the benefit of the whole world. UNESCO is one of the parts of the UN. It was set up, amongst other things, to promote and support cultural activities and education.

As part of these activities, UNESCO's World Heritage Committee decides which places can be officially named, or designated, World Heritage sites – places that are, as UNESCO states, of 'Outstanding Universal Value', so important to the world as a whole. These sites are broadly divided into two groups.

First, cultural sites created by people, which are usually historic. They can be individual buildings, from fortresses to factories. They may also be entire villages or whole cities centres.

The second group is made up of natural landscapes and geographical areas. They range from forests and deserts to caves and waterfalls. These areas may be important because of the plants and animals they contain. Some sites fall into both the natural and cultural categories.

THE ACROPOLIS, ATHENS

The Acropolis is a cultural World Heritage site of ancient Greece, famous for its beautiful temple complex. It lies at the centre of Athens, the city considered to be the birthplace of democracy.

HERITAGE

UNESCO SAYS

Heritage is our legacy from the past, what we live with today, and what we pass on to future generations. Our cultural and natural heritage are both irreplaceable sources of life and inspiration ... World Heritage sites belong to all the peoples of the world, irrespective of the territory on which they are located.

IN NUMBERS

1,154 World Heritage sites in total
897 Cultural sites
218 Natural sites
39 Mixed cultural and natural sites
52 World Heritage sites in danger

SAGARMATHA NATIONAL PARK

This park is a natural World Heritage Site in Nepal. Its spectacular landscape is dominated by Mount Everest (Sagarmatha), the world's highest mountain at 8,848m.

CHAPTER 1: OUR WORLD HERITAGE

HOW IT ALL BEGAN

During the 1960s, people grew more aware of the dangers to our world heritage from both nature and human activity. They realised that certain places needed protection. Two campaigns to save important sites gained international attention. This led to the idea of the 'World Heritage sites' being developed in the 1970s.

DEVELOPMENT VERSUS HERITAGE

In 1960, Egypt began to build the Aswan High Dam on the River Nile. The dam was needed to protect the Nile valley from flooding and to generate electricity. Lake Nasser, the artificial lake (or reservoir) created by the dam, would also help feed Egypt's growing population by providing water to irrigate their crops.

However, Lake Nasser threatened to flood 22 ancient monuments, including the famous temple of Abu Simbel. In 1960, UNESCO launched its 'Nubia Campaign' to save the temples and monuments, calling for international technical and financial help to move the monuments.

It took 20 years to move all the sites. The relocation of Abu Simbel was a spectacular engineering achievement (see left), taking four and a half years and costing US$42 million. Described as 'the greatest archaeological rescue operation of all time', the campaign started a new, international approach to saving world heritage.

TIMELINE

1945
UNESCO is created by 37 nations at a post-war conference in London, UK.

1960
The Nubia Campaign to save the temple of Abu Simbel in Egypt is launched.

1966
Venice is badly flooded, leading to the creation of the Venice Campaign.

1972
An international treaty, the Convention Concerning the Protection of the World Cultural and Natural Heritage, is agreed.

NATURAL DISASTER

In 1966, floods overwhelmed the historic city of Venice, Italy (see above). The water damaged buildings, art treasures and over one million books and manuscripts. The floods also alerted the world that much of Venice was badly neglected and in need of repair.

This led to international action to raise money, and groups were set up, such as the Venice in Peril Fund in London and Save Venice in New York, which still operate today.

UNESCO launched an International Safeguarding Appeal and worked to bring together fundraising efforts around the world. The campaign marked another step on the way to establishing a World Heritage List.

1977
The World Heritage Committee meets for the first time in Paris, France.

1978
The first 12 World Heritage sites are listed. The World Heritage emblem is designed.

1992
The World Heritage Centre is set up to manage the World Heritage List and support individual countries.

2021
Over 1,100 sites in 167 countries are listed as World Heritage sites.

THE FIRST WORLD HERITAGE SITES

The first list of World Heritage sites was agreed at an international meeting in Washington, DC, USA, in 1978. Just 12 sites in seven countries were on the original List, compared to 1,154 in 167 countries today. Even at this stage some of the main trends of the future were clear, for example the variety of sites.

L'ANSE AUX MEADOWS HISTORIC VIKING SITE, CANADA

Discovered in 1960, the remains of this camp provided evidence of the first European settlement in the Americas in the 11th century CE. Previously people had thought Europeans only reached North America in the late 15th century.

NAHANNI NATIONAL PARK RESERVE, CANADA

This huge national park was listed for its spectacular geographical features including river canyons, hot springs and cave systems. It is home to the Virginia Falls, one of North America's highest waterfalls.

YELLOWSTONE NATIONAL PARK, USA

Yellowstone is most famous for its geysers, a type of hot spring found in volcanic areas. Two-thirds of all the geysers on Earth are found there. The park is a refuge for rare animal species including bison.

MESA VERDE NATIONAL PARK, USA

Mesa Verde, in Colorado, is listed because of its ancient Pueblo Indian houses, usually built into the rock cliffs. Over 4,300 archaeological sites have been discovered in the park. The Pueblo culture lasted for 900 years, from 450 to 1300.

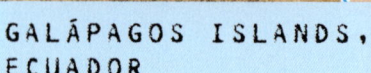

GALÁPAGOS ISLANDS, ECUADOR

The 127 islands of the Galápagos lie 1,000 km from the continent of South America. Thanks to their isolation, many unique species of animal life developed here. British scientist Charles Darwin formed his theory of evolution after a visit to the Galápagos in 1835.

CITY OF QUITO, ECUADOR

The capital of Ecuador, Quito, has the best-preserved historic centre of any city in South America. It was founded by Spanish colonists in 1534 and is packed with old churches and mansion houses.

AACHEN CATHEDRAL, GERMANY

Aachen Cathedral grew up around a beautiful chapel, built between 793 and 813 CE for the Emperor Charlemagne, who ruled much of western Europe. He was buried here in 814. The cathedral's architecture inspired many later church buildings in western Europe.

ROYAL SALT MINES, POLAND

One of Europe's earliest industrial sites, the Royal Salt Mines show how mining has developed from the 13th to the 20th century. The site includes underground chapels, workshops and storehouses.

UNESCO SAYS

The World Heritage emblem is used to identify properties protected by the World Heritage Convention and inscribed on the official World Heritage List ... Designed by Belgian artist Michel Olyff, it was adopted as the official emblem of the World Heritage Convention in 1978. While the central square symbolises the results of human skill and inspiration, the circle celebrates the gifts of nature. The emblem is round, like the world, a symbol of global protection for the heritage of all humankind.

HISTORIC CENTRE OF KRAKOW, POLAND

Krakow's historic centre dates from the 13th century. It includes hundreds of palaces, churches and merchants' houses. Important monuments include the cathedral, Wawel Castle, old city walls, the Jagiellonian University and the large medieval market square.

SIMIEN NATIONAL PARK, ETHIOPIA

Simien National Park was listed for two reasons: its unique mountain and canyon landscape (caused by erosion) and its variety of life (biodiversity). The Park is home to rare species of wolves, goats, baboons and vultures.

ISLAND OF GORÉE, SENEGAL

The little island of Gorée, just off the coast of Senegal, was a centre of the slave trade between Africa and the Americas from 1536 to 1848. The site includes a fortress and the House of Slaves, where enslaved people were locked up.

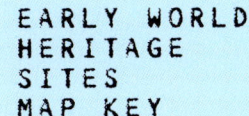

ROCK-HEWN CHURCHES OF LALIBELA, ETHIOPIA

These 11 churches were carved out of solid rock in the 12th century, a unique method of construction. It was a place of pilgrimage for African Christians unable to travel to Jerusalem, and so became known as 'New Jerusalem'.

EARLY WORLD HERITAGE SITES MAP KEY

- 🔵 Natural site
- 🔶 Cultural site

CHAPTER 1 : OUR WORLD HERITAGE

ON THE DANGER LIST

AUSTRIA – historic city centre of Vienna, threatened by modern high-rise construction.

USA – Everglades, Florida, in danger due to water pollution, urban development and rising sea levels caused by climate change.

A World Heritage site is, by definition, in need of protection and preservation. However, as early as 1979, a new list was added to work alongside the World Heritage List. It is called 'World Heritage in Danger'. It highlights sites that are under serious threat and aims to trigger action to protect them. It also helps raise additional money to fund this action.

DEMOCRATIC REPUBLIC OF THE CONGO – four rainforest sites, some home to endangered gorillas, are on the Danger List, due to poaching, illegal logging, mining and armed conflict

WORLD HERITAGE IN DANGER MAP KEY
- 🔵 Natural site
- 🔶 Cultural site

10

The main aim of UNESCO's Danger List is to work towards a point where a site can come off it! The town of Kotor in Montenegro (formerly Yugoslavia) was the first site to be placed on the Danger List in 1979, after an earthquake destroyed or damaged many historic buildings and monuments. After many years of restoration work, Kotor was removed from the Danger List in 2003.

In 1990 there were just seven sites on the Danger List, but by 2000 the number had grown to 30. Today, 52 sites are on the Danger List – 36 cultural sites and 16 natural sites. Some 70 per cent of sites in danger are located in Africa and the Arab States. This is due to a high level of armed conflict at various times in the past 20 years. Some countries feel it is a sign of failure for one of their sites to be listed as 'In Danger'. But in the long run this is one of the best ways to help save a site.

SYRIA – six historic cultural sites, including the Ancient City of Aleppo, on the Danger List, due to armed conflict.

INDONESIA – tropical rainforest of Sumatra threatened by poaching, logging and road building.

LIBYA – five historic cultural sites on the Danger List, due to armed conflict.

Because of their nature, nearly all sites on the World Heritage List are under some kind of threat, whether or not they are placed on the Danger List. At least one of the 'dangers' (see panel) can be found almost everywhere that heritage sites are located. Many cultural sites are very old, and this puts them at risk as well. In the coming pages, we will look at the work to save all World Heritage sites, not just those on the Danger List.

MAIN DANGERS FOR SITES

- Urban development
- Armed conflict
- Environmental factors (e.g. climate change)
- Industrial and agricultural development
- Lack of planning for conservation

CHAPTER 2: HERITAGE IN

A place becomes a World Heritage site through an official recognition process, called 'designation'. This process is run by UNESCO and agreed by its members (countries). But it is essential for the success of this process that local people and communities support it and are involved in managing the site.

DESIGNATING A WORLD HERITAGE SITE

- A country selects a place to be designated as a World Heritage site.
- It prepares information about this site and submits it to UNESCO.
- UNESCO experts examine the submission to make sure a site is globally important, having 'Outstanding Universal Value'.
- An approved submission is put forward to the World Heritage Committee, consisting of 21 members elected by different countries, to vote on.
- If they agree to a designation, the site is added to the World Heritage List.

ACTION

UNESCO does not own any sites. Within a historic city centre site, there may be privately owned houses and office buildings owned by companies. Religious organisations may own churches, mosques and temples. Some heritage sites, such as castles and historic houses, are owned and managed by the state. Others are maintained by Non-Governmental Organisations (NGOs), associations and charities, such as the National Trust in Great Britain.

Natural sites are more likely to be owned by governments or public bodies. Usually they have already been protected as national parks or game reserves. However, within these protected areas, land may still be privately owned, for example by farmers. Sometimes natural sites may be on land that belongs to indigenous peoples.

OLD AND NEW TOWNS OF EDINBURGH

The Scottish capital, Edinburgh, is famous for its castle, Royal Palace, medieval Old Town and 18th-century New Town, built in a neoclassical style. These Old and New Towns were listed as a World Heritage site in 1995, but community initiatives to protect Edinburgh's heritage began in the 1960s. Volunteers, including architects and surveyors as well as fundraisers and campaigners, worked to save the New Town's buildings from falling into ruin. Since 1999, these efforts have continued under an organisation called Edinburgh World Heritage, an independent charity.

Edinburgh World Heritage involves local people in conserving the city. They may become a member of the charity, donate money or volunteer to help in conservation and education projects. The charity also trains young people. For example, apprentices can learn a trade such as stonemasonry – stonemasons have vital skills needed to restore traditional buildings, and there is currently a shortage of masons in Scotland.

CHAPTER 2 : HERITAGE IN ACTION

MEET THE HERITAGE WORKERS

Around the world, hundreds of thousands of people work to protect heritage sites. Because these sites attract millions of tourists, many jobs have been created as a result of World Heritage status. Ticket collectors, security guards, cleaners, maintenance workers, tour guides and translators are among some of those directly employed at sites. Many jobs are also created indirectly through tourism, for example hotel and restaurant workers. Some work relating to protecting heritage is particularly specialised.

HERE ARE SOME OF THE PROFESSIONS INVOLVED IN HERITAGE WORK ...

PLANNERS

Planners work to ensure that land and buildings are used in line with local regulations and government plans. They aim to balance the needs of business with those of local residents and the environment. Planners try to make sure that development around a heritage site does not damage it, for example by causing pollution or by spoiling views. When historic city centres are heritage sites, they try to make sure new buildings are in keeping with the historic nature of the city.

ARCHITECTS

On World Heritage sites, architects work on restoration projects to save major buildings. They use the best available technology, new and old, to preserve the building's original structure and appearance. They also work on new buildings within historic city centres or close to heritage buildings. Here, the challenge is to design modern buildings without spoiling the character of the area – and getting others to agree to them!

RESTORERS

Restorers usually work on individual historic objects, such as paintings, sculptures, furniture and books, although they may also work on entire buildings. Conservation work is very specialised and often time-consuming, taking months or even years to complete. Patience and steady hands are essential! Increasingly, technology is used in restoration, for example in computer analysis of ancient paint.

WILDLIFE RANGERS

Wildlife rangers are on the front line of protecting natural heritage sites, particularly their biodiversity and wildlife. In many parts of the world, being a ranger is a dangerous occupation. Since 2012, at least 384 rangers have been killed in Africa by poachers or illegal miners and loggers. Rangers have great knowledge of the animals and landscapes they are protecting. They work as guides for visitors to the sites. They encourage local people to protect the sites they live in, too.

TOURISM MANAGERS

Tourism is important for heritage sites because it brings money to both the site and the local area. However, it also brings many problems (see page 30). Tourism managers work to find ways to make tourism as beneficial as possible for a site. For example, they might find ways to encourage visitors through the year rather than just in the summer to reduce crowds at peak times. Some managers promote 'eco-tourism', or travel that is more respectful of the environment.

SITE MANAGERS

The site manager of a World Heritage site organises on a day-to-day basis, finds and co-ordinates the other people needed to ensure its smooth running and up-keep. Site managers are the main contact between sites and the World Heritage Centre.

HISTORIANS

Understanding the history of a heritage site is vital for its preservation. During restoration, historians research a site's past to help return a building to its original state. They find clues in old documents about past building techniques and plans, so as to advise restorers and architects. Historians also present information to the public who visit sites. New historical discoveries can change our understanding of why buildings were built, and how they were originally used.

ARCHAEOLOGISTS

Like historians, archaeologists look for clues to the past, but they find them in the remains of the buildings and the traces in the earth left behind by the people who lived there. Working with other scientists and historians, they try to establish what was there in the past and where it might be useful to explore more by digging.

NATURAL SCIENTISTS

Many different scientists contribute to our understanding of natural World Heritage sites: geologists uncover the processes that formed our rocks and landscapes, oceanographers study our seas, naturalists explore life on Earth and its huge variety (or biodiversity), ecologists find ways that life interacts with its surroundings. All these scientists may work as conservationists, working to protect the natural world.

CHAPTER 2: HERITAGE IN ACTION

INVOLVING THE COMMUNITY

Once a site joins the World Heritage List, involving local organisations and people is very important for its success. Active local participation in protecting a site raises public awareness and helps a community value its heritage. At a practical level, it gives people work and can train them in the skills needed to look after these special places.

The World Heritage Volunteers Programme organises action camps around the world to involve young people. Volunteers learn new skills by practical work to clean up and restore heritage sites, from temples to lagoons. Over 5,000 people have taken part so far in over 60 countries.

One group of 12 volunteers, sent to an island in the Seychelles, collected 25 tonnes of plastic waste, helping to protect endangered green turtles.

ASMARA — Eritrea

Asmara, the capital of Eritrea, is a superb example of a planned city. Hundreds of Art Deco and modernist buildings from 1893 to 1941 survive there, including hotels, cinemas, offices, schools, private houses and even a beautifully designed petrol station. Asmara was added to the World Heritage List in 2017.

Since then, UNESCO has organised workshops and training to bring together local architects and planners. The aim is to raise awareness of the need to conserve Asmara, and to help give people the skills to manage the site.

CANADA'S FIRST NATIONS

Ten of Canada's UNESCO sites are either within national parks or connected with them. Most of these have been home to Indigenous peoples (known as First Nations, Inuit and Métis in Canada) for many thousands of years.

Parks Canada run these sites, but the Indigenous people are very much involved and many work as park staff. Often Indigenous people have greater knowledge of the environment, built up over the generations, for thousands of years.

By consulting with Indigenous hunters, Parks Canada is in a better position to protect species such as caribou and seals.

HAIDA WATCHMEN

The World Heritage site of SGang Gwaay, an island off Vancouver, is home to the Haida people. Canada Parks and the Haida jointly run the site. The Haida are known for their wood carved memorial poles. At the top of some of these poles are three figures in tall hats - watchmen who protect the island.
In the summer months, local people become 'watchmen', showing visitors around their home.

Canada

THE TOMBS OF BUGANDA KINGS

Uganda

Found in Kasubi, an area of Kampala, the capital of Uganda, these large tombs are amazing constructions of grass thatch and wooden frames. Dating from the 1880s, the tombs have a great spiritual significance for the Buganda people.

In 2010 a major fire caused serious damage to the main tomb, leading the site to be placed on UNESCO's Danger List. UNESCO helped to pay for reconstruction works. As part of this, local young people were trained in traditional construction techniques by older builders. This ensures that, if there is another fire, the skills survive for restoration to take place again.

CHAPTER 3:
EXPANDING

In the last 70 years, the world's population trebled, going from 2.5 billion in 1950 to 7.8 billion in 2020. At the same time, many people have moved from rural areas to cities. Today, 56 per cent of people live in urban areas, compared to only 30 per cent in 1950. This number is expected to grow to 68 per cent by 2050. Urban development creates many challenges for protecting heritage sites.

JAIPUR CITY

The walled city of Jaipur is capital of the Indian state of Rajasthan. Founded in 1727, it was carefully planned from the start with a grid pattern of streets divided into districts, guided by both local Hindu and European ideas and built using the local pink stone. Jaipur City was named a World Heritage site in 2019. Like many cities in India today, its population is growing – it is now nearly 4 million. In 1950, it was under 300,000. The city authorities are developing strict regulations to preserve the unique style of the buildings within the old city walls.

CITIES

As cities expand, they occupy more and more of the countryside that surrounds them, putting pressure on some heritage sites. Within cities, the growth of traffic and increasing air pollution puts historic buildings at risk. Land increases in value, making it more profitable to build modern tall buildings for offices or apartments, rather than preserving low-rise older ones.

Meanwhile new construction can block out the views for which cities are famous. Instead of castles, temples or cathedrals, tall glass towers dominate skylines. Roads cut through historic areas of cities.

Protecting heritage from rapid and badly planned development can have many benefits, particularly by bringing in tourists who spend money in a country. It is also an important part of maintaining the character and culture of a city, in a world where urban areas are coming to look more and more similar. This helps people to understand the history of their own city.

It is not easy for governments to balance heritage and the economy. UNESCO provides advice on ways of doing this. The World Heritage Centre will also object to planned changes if it feels it will damage a heritage site. In 2009, it took the Dresden Elbe Valley off the List because of the decision to build a bridge over the Elbe River, which flows through Dresden.

UNESCO felt the bridge would bring too much traffic into the historic city and spoil the beauty of the Elbe Valley. UNESCO suggested building a tunnel instead. The German authorities felt the economic benefits of building the bridge outweighed its impact on the area's heritage.

CHAPTER 3: EXPANDING CITIES

BUILDING UP THREATS

No one expects a place to stay unchanged over time. City planners and heritage managers alike recognise that a city is a living thing and will not survive if it simply becomes a museum. At the same time, cities contain precious history. It is important that these heritage sites are not only protected, but that the buildings that grow up around them do not overwhelm them and look right alongside their older neighbours, both close up and from afar.

LIVERPOOL – MARITIME MERCANTILE CITY

Six areas of Liverpool in England became part of a World Heritage site in 2004, in recognition of the city's status as one of the world's largest ports between the 18th and early 20th centuries. The site included its docks, some warehouses and fine stone offices of its shipping companies. In 2012 UNESCO placed the site on its Danger List because it was worried about plans to redevelop the historic dockland areas. Despite this, some of the building projects went ahead, changing the skyline. As a result, Liverpool was removed from the list of World Heritage sites in 2021.

HISTORIC CENTRE OF VIENNA

The capital of Austria, Vienna is famous for its Baroque palaces and grand 19th-century architecture. Its large old centre is a World Heritage site. The Viennese value their heritage and it is well protected by local regulations. However, plans for an office block and a new hotel complex in the city centre have caused controversy because of their visual impact on the old city landscape (left is a designer's image of how it might look). The World Heritage Committee has placed Vienna on its Danger List while the plans are reviewed.

SAMARKAND – CROSSROAD OF CULTURES

Samarkand in Uzbekistan was an important city on the ancient Silk Route across Central Asia from China to Europe. Many different peoples have met to exchange goods in its markets. The city's beautifully decorated mosques and houses have made it a World Heritage site. The city needs new roads and more space to accommodate the tourists that visit, so UNESCO is watching the plans closely and working with the government of Uzbekistan to make sure these developments do not invade the city's heritage.

QUÉBEC PLANNERS

The city of Québec in Canada dates from the 17th century and it still has many buildings and fortifications dating from that time. Its historic district became a World Heritage site in 1985 and many of its 1,400 buildings have since been restored. Working together, the local, state and national governments have developed initiatives where private owners have been given money to restore their properties and ordinary citizens are involved in planning decisions. People who live in Québec feel very attached to their city and its heritage.

SPREADING OUTWARDS

Preventing urban sprawl is one of UNESCO's key challenges. Often heritage sites are found on the edge of big cities, which are spreading rapidly outwards. This threatens precious landscapes nearby. Some of these fast-growing cities are found in poorer countries, where daily life can be challenging for many people. A government may feel that supporting its people is more important than preserving its heritage, but increasingly, planners are realising that protecting heritage helps a city to prosper.

RIO DE JANEIRO LANDSCAPES

Watched over by the statue of Christ on Corcovado Mountain, the spectacular landscape that surrounds Rio de Janeiro, Brazil, has shaped the city and contributed to its unique, vibrant culture. In 2012 this landscape was listed as a huge World Heritage site, taking in both natural and built heritage, from mountains and beaches to elegant parks and reclaimed land.

The World Heritage status supports the on-going plan to protect this huge site, which is very important for tourism and the economic success of the city. There are controls on tall buildings and buffer zones to prevent new development on the mountainsides. However, it is hard to control the construction of illegal housing and the city's dense population causes water pollution.

EVERGLADES NATIONAL PARK

These unique coastal wetlands are found at the tip of Florida, USA. They have a rich biodiversity, with alligators, many species of wading birds and the rare manatee. The Everglades has been a World Heritage site since 1979 but is now, for the second time, on the Danger List because of the pollution, from the nearby urban development and agriculture (see pages 26–27), of the fresh water that creates its ecosystem. This has long been a problem – the Everglades were made a national park in 1947 to protect the area, as over 50 per cent had already been lost to growing cities, such as Orlando.

HISTORIC AREAS OF ISTANBUL

From Roman times, Istanbul has always been one of the world's largest cities. Its position on the border between Europe and Asia makes it a bridge between the two. It is packed with amazing buildings from early churches to Ottoman palaces. In 1985, when the historic parts of Istanbul were made a World Heritage site, it was already home to 5.5 million people.

Today, 15.2 million live in this Turkish megacity. According to UNESCO, the monuments of Istanbul are under threat from 'population pressure, industrial pollution and uncontrolled urbanisation'. The Turkish government is now spending money to restore historic buildings and to create new public transport systems that will reduce congestion and cut pollution.

EVERGLADES NATURAL SCIENTISTS

Ecologists have realised that by protecting the fresh water habitats of the Everglades, they are also conserving a vital resource for the people who live in the area. People need water to live, too. Their research has encouraged the US government to invest in new water systems in the area. These systems will help sustain both the Everglades biodiversity and the cities that surround them.

CHAPTER 4: BUSINESS

As the number of people on Earth has grown, so have all the activities needed to feed them and provide them with the goods they buy. As people have got wealthier in the last 50 years, they consume more, including cars and electronic goods. The increase of fishing, farming and industry has huge benefits for people, but it also threatens the environment, including many natural World Heritage sites.

IN NUMBERS

In the past **50** years:
- Over **11** per cent of global species have been lost
- Mining extractions have more than tripled

In the past **30** years:
- Sustainable fish stocks fell from **90** to **65** per cent
- **10** per cent of forests have been cleared

OR BEAUTY?

To resource human activity, Earth's forests are being cut down and seas are being cleared of fish. Mining for metals – necessary for phones and batteries, for example – has a terrible impact on biodiversity and is speeding up climate change (see page 42). Water is increasingly a scarce resource, too, because mining, industry, farming and growing populations use so much of it.

UNESCO and environmental groups try to encourage businesses to balance the demands of economic growth with a healthy environment – a balance known as sustainability. Today there is growing pressure from consumers for companies to make their products sustainably. Farmers are asked to consider the environment rather than just producing more. Governments too are under pressure to act to protect Earth's resources and to encourage recycling and re-use of products.

There are some positive results. For example, with strong laws to control the ocean's fisheries, some fish populations are beginning to rise again after years of decline.

Natural heritage sites only cover a small proportion of our planet, but they show that a different way of doing things is possible. Protecting natural heritage sites, such as rainforests, is one way to fight climate change and reduce the impact of mining and forestry. Around 30 per cent of the world's rainforests are now protected in some way.

LAKE BAIKAL

The oldest and deepest lake in the world, Lake Baikal in Siberia, Russia, holds 20 per cent of the world's fresh water. Baikal has a special significance for Russians, and it is said that swimming in the ice-cold lake will add extra years to a person's life. The great biodiversity of the lake includes freshwater seals and rare fish species. However, Lake Baikal is also in the heart of Siberia, a vast region important for its oil, timber and mineral resources. These are vital for the economy of Russia.

Pollution of the lake, illegal timber harvesting, tourism, papermills and the building of oil and gas pipelines nearby are all threats to this unique environment. Protests by environmental groups have managed to get a pipeline re-routed and a papermill closed down.

CHAPTER 4 : BUSINESS OR BEAUTY?

FISHING AND FARMING

Fishing and farming feed the world's people and, as the population grows, inevitably this puts pressure on our land and oceans. In addition, global diets have changed, and people eat much more meat and fish than 50 years ago. Overfishing is a problem in many of the world's oceans, and the expansion of animal farming often destroys rainforests.

Mexico Brazil
Ecuador

THE WHALE SANCTUARY OF EL VIZCAÍNO

This World Heritage site in Mexico is a protected area of sea that has been listed by UNESCO since 1993. Its remote coastal lagoons are where Pacific grey whales breed, but they are also home to a large salt industry. Salt is very important in food production. In 1999, a new salt works was proposed which would have threatened the breeding ground of the whales. Thanks to pressure from heritage campaigners, the Mexican government stopped the salt works project from going ahead.

THE GALÁPAGOS ISLANDS

These islands off the coast of Ecuador are most famous for their rare onshore species. They are also at the centre of a huge marine reserve in the Pacific Ocean. Even though these waters are protected, there has been an upsurge of illegal fishing by large boats from around the world. One fishing boat was stopped with 6,000 sharks on board – including some protected species. Some fishing boats stay just outside the reserve, but this still reduces fish stocks inside it. UNESCO is urging other countries to support Ecuador in stopping this illegal fishing, which goes against international agreements.

THE AMAZON RAINFOREST

The decline of the vast Amazon tropical rainforest due to human activity is one of the greatest environment threats to Earth. UNESCO, along with NGOs and individuals, campaigns to protect the Amazon at local and international levels. Several countries have designated parts of the Amazon as World Heritage sites – Brazil, Colombia, Ecuador, Peru and Suriname. This provides some protection, but only a small part of the Amazon rainforest is covered in this way.

The forests are cleared by logging and mining (see page 28) as well as for farming, in particular to create grazing for beef cattle. The loss of the rainforest threatens biodiversity, rare species and the homelands of indigenous peoples. Rainforests are often described as the lungs of our planet – they absorb the carbon dioxide gas that is contributing to global warming and give out oxygen. Turning forest into farmland contributes to climate change.

In Brazil in particular, the demand for meat, wood, iron ore and other products of mining – and the profits these bring – is prioritised over conserving the rainforest. Road building and the growth of cities only add to the problems.

CHAPTER 4: BUSINESS OR BEAUTY?

MINING AND LOGGING

Mining and logging have been shaping landscapes around the world for thousands of years. Sometimes these activities have created World Heritage sites we celebrate today.

As these industries have grown, their negative effects on the environment are raising concerns. Drilling for oil and gas, since the late 19th century, has added to the problems.

CITY OF POTOSÍ

YELLOWSTONE NATIONAL PARK

USA

High in the Andes Mountains of Bolivia, Potosí has been the home of silver mines since the 16th century. The wealth this earned led to a city of beautiful Baroque buildings, whilst the miners created a remarkable irrigation system via aqueducts and artificial lakes. In 1987 both the old city and the historic mines were declared a World Heritage site.

In 2014, the site was put on the Danger List. Mining continues in the area and the mountain on which Potosí is built is in danger of collapsing. The industry pollutes water supplies, too. The mines are now less rich in silver, but people continue to dig them in dangerous conditions, as it is an important way for local residents to make a living. Despite many problems, the government is trying to protect the mountain and some historic buildings have been restored. UNESCO is supporting this work.

Yellowstone, with its grizzly bears and geysers, is the most well-known protected area in the USA. Mining is not allowed within the park, but companies are keen to mine for gold just outside it, threatening its wildlife and landscape. There are regular arguments about mining in the region. Local residents and environmental organisations have now persuaded the US government to stop mining in the area.

Bolivia

ARABIAN ORYX SANCTUARY

In 1982, a sanctuary was created in the desert of Oman to provide a reserve for the rare Arabian oryx, a type of antelope which had become extinct in the wild. The area later became a World Heritage site. In 2006, the government of Oman decided to reduce the size of the site by 90 per cent, in order to allow drilling for oil and gas. As a result, the Arabian Oryx Sanctuary became the first ever site to be removed from the World Heritage List. The number of oryx living in the reserve, which had recovered to about 450, fell to 61 by 2011. The oryx is a symbol of Oman, sometimes known as its 'national animal'.

BEECH FORESTS OF THE CARPATHIANS

The beech forests of Europe date back to the Ice Age and include a 1,500 square km area that stretches along the Carpathian Mountains. They provide a unique environment for many different animals, from wolves to golden eagles. This ancient habitat was given World Heritage status in 2007, and now includes areas found in 18 different countries.

The biggest threat to the forests comes from illegal logging, as beechwood is valuable. Environmental organisations are working to raise awareness of the problem. Sometimes forestry workers who try to stop logging are attacked. The European Union (EU) is taking action against Romania for failing to stop illegal logging on its territory.

CHAPTER 5:
HERE COME

Tourism has grown massively in the last 70 years. In 1950, there were just 25 million tourists. By 2018 there were 1.4 billion, over 50 times more. Whilst in 1950, nearly all tourists were from Europe and North America, now many others travel. In 2019, the largest number of tourists – 155 million – came from China. The Covid-19 crisis may have changed these global travel patterns, but it has also highlighted both the benefits and problems tourism brings.

THE TOURISTS

World Heritage sites attract huge numbers of tourists – particularly the historic cities of Europe and ancient monuments worldwide. Being recognised as a World Heritage site nearly always increases the number of visitors. Countries and cities welcome this because it brings in money and helps create jobs. Millions of people work in hotels, restaurants, as tour guides and in shops aimed at tourists.

But the visitors bring problems. The sheer numbers put pressure on structures, from simple wear and tear to large-scale erosion. More roads, buildings and infrastructure are needed to accommodate the visitors, and this adds to pollution. Old monuments or remote landscapes are particularly vulnerable. Wildlife is also threatened. In addition, local people can suffer from increased tourism. Prices can go up, transport systems become overcrowded and housing more expensive. Their traditional culture and way of life may be put under pressure. This is why more and more countries are seeking to achieve 'sustainable' tourism. This means controlling visitor numbers, protecting the environment and educating tourists about how to respect local cultures. UNESCO provides help and support in achieving these goals to safeguard world heritage.

VENICE, ITALY

Venice in Italy (see pages 6–7) today has up to 25 million tourists every year, which puts huge pressure on its ancient buildings. In 2017 UNESCO considered placing the city on its Danger List to protect it. Now, the city is taking steps to control visitor numbers by charging for entry. It is banning larger cruise ships. More difficult is dealing with the two-thirds fall in the historic city's permanent population since 1951, as apartments are turned into tourism rentals and ordinary shops become souvenir stores.

CHAPTER 5 : HERE COME THE TOURISTS

EUROPE'S HISTORIC CITIES

Europe's historic cities are home to many World Heritage sites including many whole historic centres. People visit these places for short city breaks, which are growing much faster than traditional beach holidays. Europe is home to half of all tourist arrivals in the world – 746 million in 2019. The interruption of this travel by Covid-19 has been seen as an opportunity for Europe's 'museum cities' to rethink their approach to visitors.

THESE ARE SOME OF THE NEGATIVE EFFECTS OF CITY TOURISM IDENTIFIED BY UNESCO REPORTS:

- Road congestion
- Crowded public transport
- Economic losses from empty second homes
- Raised house prices
- Pressure on hospitals and other public services
- Plastic pollution
- Souvenir hunters damaging monuments
- Disorderly behaviour
- Air pollution caused by cruise ships and motor traffic

AMSTERDAM'S 17TH-CENTURY CANAL RING

HERE ARE HOW THREE EUROPEAN CITY WORLD HERITAGE SITES ARE ADDRESSING SOME OF THESE PROBLEMS ...

Amsterdam grew up around its unique canal network, as it became wealthy trading around the world. Today, tourists enjoy canal trips and admire its old houses. But in 2018, 19 million visitors overwhelmed its 850,000 residents. Some inhabitants have moved out of the city centre, whilst others have to tolerate rowdy, late-night parties.

The Dutch government has started an 'Enjoy and Respect' campaign for the city: tourists are fined for bad behaviour, a ban has been put on building new hotels and tourist taxes have been increased. The campaign encourages people to visit other parts of the Netherlands.

Europe

OLD CITY OF DUBROVNIK

Known as the 'Pearl of the Adriatic', the walled city of Dubrovnik in Croatia became an important Mediterranean port from the 13th century. UNESCO is organising a major restoration programme of its beautiful old buildings.

However, the city has seen an explosion in tourist numbers, partly due to its role in the TV series *Game of Thrones*. Hundreds of cruise ships dock every year. Tourists damage the limestone streets of the old town, and two-thirds of residents have left. After UNESCO raised concerns, the city decided to limit cruise ship arrivals to two per day, with a maximum of 5,000 visitors. Cameras count the number of people entering and leaving.

HISTORIC CENTRE OF PRAGUE

Dating back to the 11th century, the old streets and bridges of Prague, capital of the Czech Republic, attract over 7 million tourists every year. Most are concentrated in the small old town. Residents suffer from the noise and nuisance of 'party tourism', fuelled by low-cost flights. The city has tried to spread visitors out into other parts of the city, to get a better balance between neighbourhoods. It has put new taxes on holiday apartment rentals.

CHAPTER 5 : HERE COME THE TOURISTS

MONUMENTS UNDER PRESSURE

A small number of great monuments created by past civilisations have become so famous that they are known around the world. These sites draw in huge numbers of visitors.

The great age of many monumental sites means that it is already a challenge to protect them from the weather, erosion and pollution. Tourists add to the difficulties. Human footfall, touching and sitting wears away a site's ancient stones. Visitors need facilities such as toilets and restaurants. Putting in the infrastructure, be it drains or electrics, to support these, may damage the site. And people simply getting to and from the site adds to pollution.

THE GREAT WALL

Built continuously from the 3rd century BCE to the 17th century CE to protect China's border, the Great Wall is over 20,000 km long, the largest defence against invasion ever constructed. By 2000, up to one-third of it had already disappeared through weathering, erosion, and theft of the stones for building materials.

Now tourists add to the problem. A single section of the wall at Badaling near Beijing attracted 9.9 million visitors in 2018. Over the past 20 years the Chinese government has worked with heritage organisations to restore and protect what remains of the Wall. This now includes a daily visitor limit of 65,000 people.

Cambodia

ANGKOR

Angkor in Cambodia is home to immense Hindu and Buddhist temple complexes dating between the 9th and 15th centuries – most famously, the temple of Angkor Wat. After civil war and large-scale theft of its art treasures, UNESCO placed the site on its Danger List between 1992 and 2004, carrying out successful conservation efforts.

However, in 2018, over 2.6 million tourists crowded into the temple sites. Visitors put the temples at risk, but their entrance fees help to pay for continuing conservation work. Hundreds of local people have jobs at the site. To control visitor numbers, the Cambodian authorities have nearly doubled the cost of visiting Angkor.

MACHU PICCHU

Peru

High in the Andes Mountains in Peru, the Inca stone city-sanctuary of Machu Picchu was built in the 15th century. Despite its remoteness, Machu Picchu is Peru's biggest tourist attraction, bringing in millions of dollars in revenue every year and creating thousands of jobs. UNESCO has repeatedly showed its concern for the preservation of the site in the face of so many visitors. This has led the Peruvian government to limit daily numbers of tourists who hike along the 'Inca Trail' to Machu Picchu.

STONEHENGE

UK

Stonehenge in England is famous for its Neolithic stone circle, built around 2500 BCE, most probably as a place of worship. Tourists began to visit from the 19th century, when they could wander freely around the site and climb onto the stones. Some even chipped away parts of the stones as souvenirs.

Gradually measures were taken to protect Stonehenge – restoring and fencing off the stones, and closing a busy road passing nearby. Today, a plan to build a road tunnel near the site to protect it from heavy traffic is causing controversy. UNESCO has raised concerns that the tunnel could damage archaeological remains that have still not been excavated.

NATURE UNDER PRESSURE

Tourists, even in small numbers, threaten natural landscapes. A World Heritage listing will attract even more people, and it is important that access to these delicate habitats is carefully managed. Simply walking through a wild area may damage its plants and animals. Local residents may welcome visitors, but will the visitors respect their beliefs and way of life?

The natural World Heritage sites are immensely varied. Some are huge, such as Yosemite National Park in the USA, while others are tiny, such as Komodo island in Indonesia with its own unique wildlife. Visitors can trample plants underfoot, drop litter that animals may then eat and create pollution through transport in and out of the parks.

KOMODO NATIONAL PARK

A population of around 5,700 giant lizards called 'Komodo dragons' inhabits these volcanic islands. They exist nowhere else in the world. A massive increase in tourists is having an impact on the habitat the dragons live in. The Indonesian government has decided to limit visitor numbers to 50,000 a year to help protect the national park.

YOSEMITE NATIONAL PARK

Yosemite National Park, California, USA is known for spectacular granite rock faces, U-shaped valleys, hidden lakes and waterfalls. This is a landscape formed by glaciation. With over 4 million visitors arriving each year, hikers on the park's trails erode the paths and damage its plants. Young adult volunteers help maintain the trails while learning about the natural world.

These remote wilderness areas have often been home to peoples whose traditional lifestyles and beliefs are built around the natural world. The Anangu people of the Uluru and Kata Tjuta National Park in Australia have worked hard to maintain their culture despite welcoming over 300,000 visitors a year. Their rangers take people on tours, explaining the spiritual significance of the park's landscape to their people.

ULURU AND KATA TJUTA NATIONAL PARK

Uluru is a single red rock or monolith towering over the sandy plain of central Australia. To its west lie the multiple rock domes of Kata Tjuta. Both are important to the ancient belief system of Anangu Aboriginals. The rocks were first known globally as Ayers Rock and the Olgas but, encouraged by UNESCO, they, and the Park they are found in, are now called by Anangu names. This recognises their traditional ownership of the land.

Australia

ANANGU BELIEFS

Anangu guides point out the western face of Uluru and tell the story of Lungkata, a greedy blue-tongue lizard who stole some other hunters' food. Dark stains on the rock suggest the fire that the hunters lit to punish him. The stains warn people not to climb the rock as this is against Anangu belief. Climbing has now been banned.

37

CHAPTER 6: IN TIMES

Disaster can strike just about anywhere in the world. It could be an earthquake, fire, flood or landslide. World Heritage sites may be badly affected by these events. Ancient buildings are fragile because of their age or how they were built. Natural sites may see their unique landscape features dramatically changed. Today, climate change adds to these threats with more extreme weather events and rising sea levels.

THE STATUE OF LIBERTY

The Statue of Liberty has been a World Heritage site since 1984. Since 1886, the colossal statue has welcomed immigrants arriving by ship from Europe to New York Harbour, coming to symbolise their hopes of freedom and a new life. In 2012, the statue was damaged by flooding caused by Hurricane Sandy. In 2016, a UNESCO climate change report highlighted that the Statue of Liberty, along with many other World Heritage sites, is at risk from climate change because of its low-lying coastal position. Plans are now being put in place to protect it from rising water levels and future severe weather events.

OF CRISIS: DISASTERS

UNESCO's World Heritage programme was developed partly in response to natural disasters. Today, when one strikes, the World Heritage Centre is on hand to encourage international aid and may also advise on and co-ordinate immediate support, working with governments, NGOs and local communities.

After the initial clean-up, it is time for long-term restoration of sites to begin. This can be very expensive and take many years. For example, after the Bam earthquake in 2003 (see page 41), the UN estimated that rebuilding would cost as much as US$1 billion. There are many different ways for this money to be raised. However, as was the case for Bam, UNESCO may place a site on the World Heritage Danger List to help raise awareness of the problems and pay for long-term solutions.

The World Heritage Centre also works to reduce the risks posed by natural disasters. It shares information to learn from previous events and how to make the best of technological development. It encourages, for example, installing fire warning systems and sprinklers, building flood protection barriers, and monitoring of ground movements in earthquake zones. At the same time, it supports local activities that will lessen the impact of a disaster, such as planting trees on hillsides to reduce the risk of landslides or combining traditional materials with stronger frames when building in an earthquake zone.

CHAPTER 6 : IN TIMES OF CRISIS: DISASTERS

FIRES, FLOODS AND EARTHQUAKES

A major disaster attracts global attention, particularly when it first happens. World Heritage status can help focus this attention. However, the challenge is not just to make the most of the instant support this generates, but also to make sure it continues during the much longer process of repairing the damage.

UNESCO monitors the reconstruction of World Heritage sites to promote best practice and to learn for the future. The world was shocked when, in April 2019, fire broke out at the famous cathedral of Notre Dame, Paris, destroying its roof and spire. Rebuilding will take many years and cost billions of Euros. The French authorities are managing the rebuild, while UNESCO is tracking the process.

Japan

SHURI-JO SITE (SHURI CASTLE)

The Shuri-jo site is one of a group of castles, known as gusuku, on Okinawa Island in Japan, dating from the Ryukyuan period (12th to 17th century). The castle, built partly of limestone and partly of wood, was heavily restored after being damaged in the Second World War.

On 31 October 2019, a fire quickly destroyed several buildings at Shuri Castle. The Japanese government immediately began planning to rebuild them. UNESCO arranged online meetings with international experts to provide advice on fire prevention measures and involved the local community. By June 2020, parts of the castle site had re-opened to visitors.

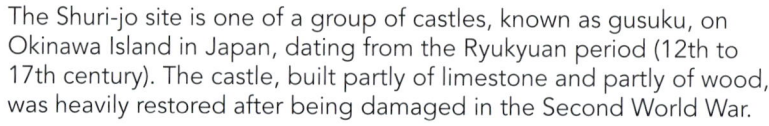

BAM

The terrible earthquake at Bam, Iran, on 26 December 2003, was first and foremost a human tragedy. More than 26,000 people were killed. Most of the city's buildings, which were made out of mud bricks in the traditional local style, collapsed. The ancient citadel, dating from the 6th to 4th centuries BCE, was flattened. Rescue specialists and relief aid poured into Iran from all over the world.

The United Nations was involved from the beginning with long-term reconstruction. Bam was placed on the UNESCO Danger List, helping to fund and plan the rebuilding initiatives. Other UN agencies gave advice on earthquake-resistant building methods. The idea was to employ the traditional building techniques using earth and mud, while also strengthening constructions against future earthquakes. By 2013 Bam was removed from the Danger List, although reconstruction continued for years afterwards.

FLORENCE

Like Venice (see pages 6–7), Florence was another historic city in Italy badly flooded in 1966, adding to the initiatives to establish a World Heritage site programme. Specialist restorers came from around the world to help dry out and clean paintings and frescoes. Volunteer helpers became known as the 'Mud Angels'.

The city has now put flood prevention plans in place to avoid a repeat of the 1966 disaster, with dams built outside the city to control water flows.

FLORENCE RESTORERS

Restoration work in Florence took time. Vasari's 16th-century masterpiece *Last Supper* was submerged in water for over 12 hours. Immediately afterwards, restorers covered it in paper to stop the paint flaking away, but it was only in 2010 that, with improved technology, they were able to start to remove the paper. Restoration finished in 2013 – nearly 50 years after the floods.

CHAPTER 6: IN TIMES OF CRISIS: DISASTERS

A CHANGING CLIMATE

Climate change happens naturally over time, but human activity is speeding up the process, with average global temperatures rising. The effects of this could be disastrous, with a rise in sea level threatening coastal areas and irregular weather patterns, including more extreme weather events, impacting the whole globe.

The World Heritage Centre has highlighted the dangers of climate change to both natural and cultural heritage. It encourages heritage sites to prepare for them. However, it also recognises that, while action can be taken at individual sites, the only real protection against the damage caused by climate change is to reduce CO_2 emissions on a global scale.

SOME OF THE NEGATIVE EFFECTS OF CLIMATE CHANGE ON WORLD HERITAGE SITES:

- Rising sea levels will flood low-lying coastal landscapes, such as lagoons, mudflats, coral reefs and islands. The world's great coastal cities, packed with heritage sites, may also be flooded. For example, London's Thames Barrier needs to be reinforced.

- Melting glaciers will change mountain landscapes, causing floods and a loss of biodiversity and natural beauty. The rivers and water supplies that the glaciers feed will also be affected.

- Extreme weather events, such as hurricanes, will damage buildings and natural landscapes.

- Biodiversity is threatened, as some species struggle to adapt to changing climate patterns. For example, 110 species of frog have become extinct in the Guanacaste Conservation Area of the Costa Rican tropical rainforests because of rising air temperatures. This has caused a fungus to grow that is deadly to the frogs.

GREAT BARRIER REEF

Australia's Great Barrier Reef is the world's largest coral reef system. It runs for 2,300 km off the coast of Queensland, in the Coral Sea. The Great Barrier Reef system includes more than 2,900 individual reefs, 900 islands and 300 coral cays (islands formed from coral). Many of the thousands of marine species living there are endangered.

Although the Reef is heavily protected and has been a UNESCO World Heritage site since 1981, it faces many threats. Farming chemicals flowing into the sea cause the most damage to water quality. Oil spills from passing ships, and tourist and port developments are also problems. Climate change is adding to these threats. Rising sea temperatures are contributing to the 'bleaching' of the coral, when the coral sheds colourful algae that lives on it and protects it from disease. As a result, more than half the Reef's coral has died since 1985.

Rising sea levels are eroding islands and cays, and in the future many may be submerged altogether. Losing corals reefs removes the habitat of many marine species and threatens biodiversity. Ironically, it also undermines the local tourism industry on which many jobs depend.

To combat coral bleaching, action is being taken to reduce other forms of pollution, improve water quality and stop excessive fishing – this all helps the coral structures to be in a better position to resist bleaching.

Australia

CHAPTER 7: IN TIMES HUMAN

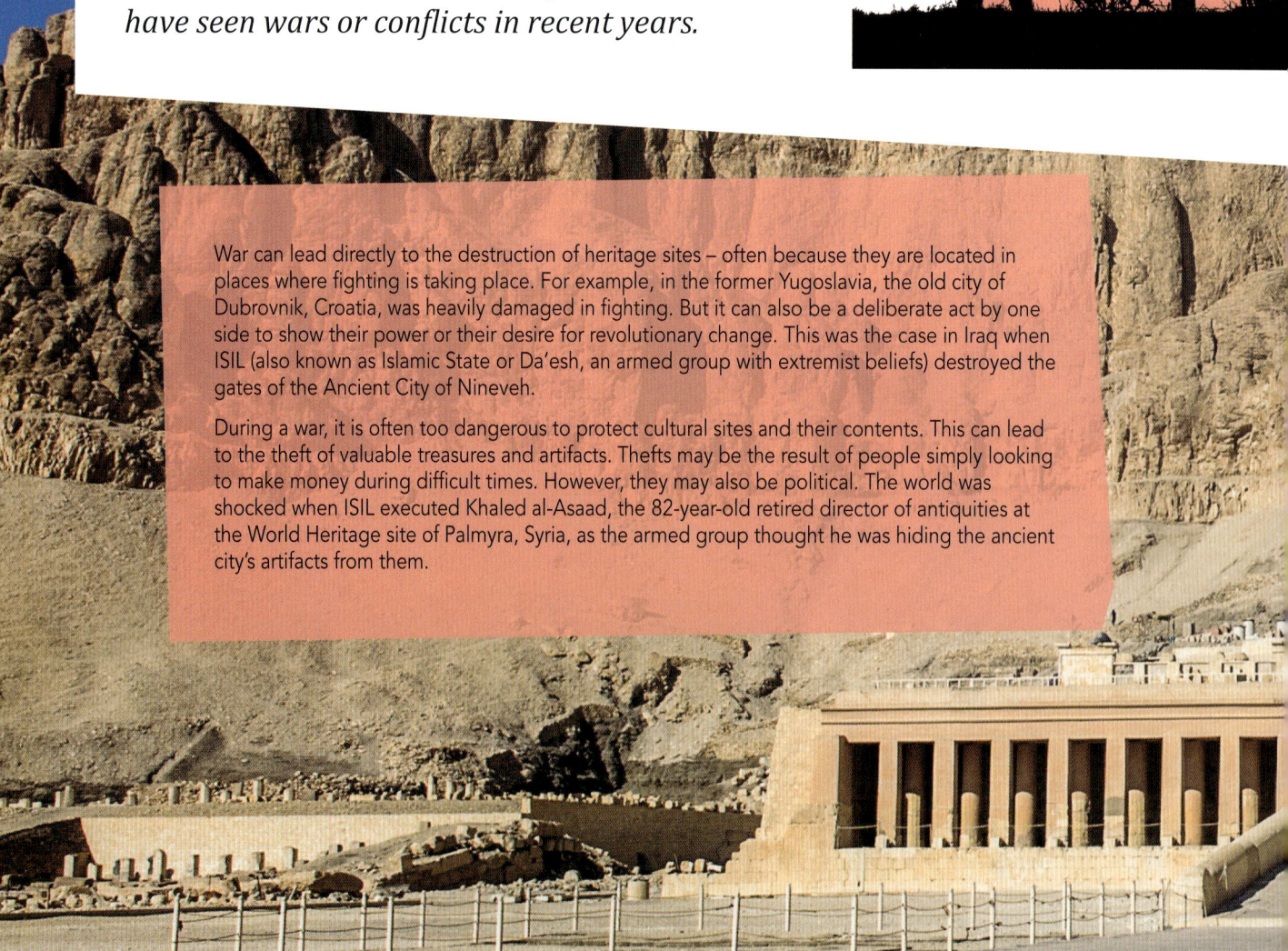

Armed conflict, including war, civil unrest and terrorism, is one of the greatest threats to our world heritage. Inevitably, in these situations, the governments and groups involved are focused on military issues. Simply feeding the population and providing medical care may become difficult. Protecting heritage, whether buildings or rainforests, is no longer a priority.

More than half of all World Heritage sites in danger are located in a small number of countries that have seen wars or conflicts in recent years.

War can lead directly to the destruction of heritage sites – often because they are located in places where fighting is taking place. For example, in the former Yugoslavia, the old city of Dubrovnik, Croatia, was heavily damaged in fighting. But it can also be a deliberate act by one side to show their power or their desire for revolutionary change. This was the case in Iraq when ISIL (also known as Islamic State or Da'esh, an armed group with extremist beliefs) destroyed the gates of the Ancient City of Nineveh.

During a war, it is often too dangerous to protect cultural sites and their contents. This can lead to the theft of valuable treasures and artifacts. Thefts may be the result of people simply looking to make money during difficult times. However, they may also be political. The world was shocked when ISIL executed Khaled al-Asaad, the 82-year-old retired director of antiquities at the World Heritage site of Palmyra, Syria, as the armed group thought he was hiding the ancient city's artifacts from them.

OF CRISIS: CONFLICT

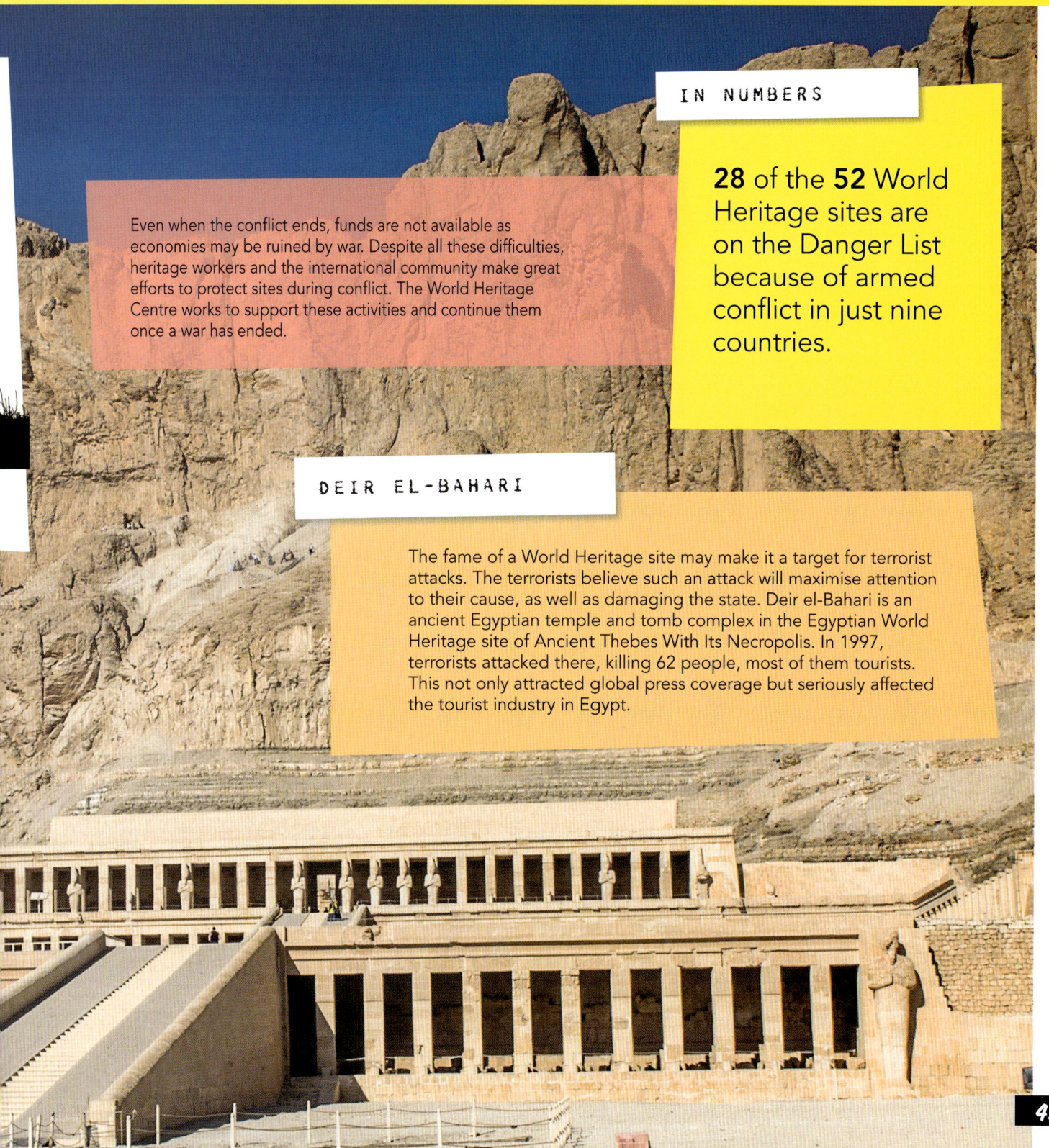

Even when the conflict ends, funds are not available as economies may be ruined by war. Despite all these difficulties, heritage workers and the international community make great efforts to protect sites during conflict. The World Heritage Centre works to support these activities and continue them once a war has ended.

IN NUMBERS

28 of the **52** World Heritage sites are on the Danger List because of armed conflict in just nine countries.

DEIR EL-BAHARI

The fame of a World Heritage site may make it a target for terrorist attacks. The terrorists believe such an attack will maximise attention to their cause, as well as damaging the state. Deir el-Bahari is an ancient Egyptian temple and tomb complex in the Egyptian World Heritage site of Ancient Thebes With Its Necropolis. In 1997, terrorists attacked there, killing 62 people, most of them tourists. This not only attracted global press coverage but seriously affected the tourist industry in Egypt.

CHAPTER 7: IN TIMES OF CRISIS: HUMAN CONFLICT

CONFLICT IN SYRIA

Two thousand years ago, many travellers along the ancient Silk Roads, which joined East with West, finished their journey on the Eastern Mediterranean coast in what is now Syria. Its ancient cities are some of the most continuously inhabited settlements in the world.

Due to Syria's location, many different peoples have settled in its land. This has led to wonderful cultural exchange but is also one of the causes of armed conflict. Since 2011, fighting has raged in Syria. As a result, all six of that country's World Heritage sites are on the Danger List.

1. CRAC DES CHEVALIERS AND QAL'AT SALAH EL-DIN

These two great castles are outstanding examples of fortified buildings. The Crac des Chevaliers was built by Crusaders in the 12th century. The Qal'at Salah El-Din (Fortress of Saladin) dates to the 10th century. Crac des Chevaliers was so strongly built that it was sadly used by modern fighters in the conflict.

2. ANCIENT CITY OF DAMASCUS

Damascus was founded in the 3rd millennium BCE and was a flourishing centre for crafts in the Middle Ages. The 8th-century Great Mosque of the Umayyads is one of its most famous sites. The conflict caused damage to parts of the old centre of Damascus.

3. ANCIENT CITY OF BOSRA

Bosra was once the capital of the Roman province of Arabia and an important stopover on the ancient caravan route to Mecca. A magnificent 2nd-century Roman theatre, early Christian ruins and several mosques are found within its walls. The Roman theatre was damaged by bombs and shells during the conflict, and the site was looted.

One of these sites, the Ancient City of Aleppo, saw some of the worst fighting of the armed conflict, including through airshelling. The collapse of the minaret of its Great Mosque, which had stood for 900 years, was a symbol of the destruction. Thousands of people died. Saving lives was everyone's priority. But the people of Aleppo are also immensely proud of their heritage and many took great risks to help preserve it.

6. ANCIENT CITY OF ALEPPO

4. SITE OF PALMYRA

5. ANCIENT VILLAGES OF NORTHERN SYRIA

Found in the centre of the modern city, ancient Aleppo has been inhabited for over 4,000 years. From the 2nd millennium BCE, it was ruled by the Hittites, Assyrians, Arabs, Mongols, Mamelukes and Ottomans. The 13th-century citadel, 12th-century Great Mosque and various 17th-century palaces, caravanserais and hammams all form part of today's unique city.

An oasis in the Syrian desert, Palmyra was one of the most important cultural centres of the ancient world. Its art and architecture combined Graeco-Roman techniques with local traditions and Persian influences. The destruction of large parts of ancient Palmyra by ISIL in 2015 was a terrible episode of the conflict. Many buildings were blown up. Quick action by local staff managed to save some artifacts from Palmyra's museum, but others were smashed or looted. Restoring Palmyra needs a lot of effort and resources.

These 40 ancient villages date from 1st to 7th centuries CE. They were abandoned in the 8th to 10th centuries but their ruins reflect the arts and culture of late Roman and Byzantine people who built them. Unfortunately, the armed conflict has damaged several sites. Many archaeological stones were illegally used as building materials – an indirect effect of the conflict.

CHAPTER 7 : IN TIMES OF CRISIS: HUMAN CONFLICT

CONFLICT IN THE RAINFORESTS

The Democratic Republic of the Congo (DRC) is a huge country, the second largest in Africa. After the Amazon, it has the largest rainforest area in the world. These forests, as well as DRC's mountain and savannah landscapes, are home to many rare animal species. Five of the country's national parks have been made into World Heritage sites.

Unfortunately, wars in DRC between 1994 and 2003 led UNESCO to place all five national parks on the Danger List. Lower levels of armed conflict have continued since 2003. Because of this and also poverty in the country, many people poach for money or try to kill endangered animals simply for their meat. It is difficult to protect endangered animals from hunters in these circumstances. Armed rebels, too, have attacked and sometimes killed park staff to steal food and fuel.

These heritage sites contain mineral resources, such as copper, diamonds, gold, coltan and cobalt. Some of these are prized as they are used in the production of mobile phones. Because DRC is a poor country, there is pressure to mine for these materials in protected areas.

1. GARAMBA NATIONAL PARK

Northern white rhinos used to live here, but due to poaching for their horns they are now extinct in the wild. Today, Garamba's rangers try to protect the park's animals from poachers, who shoot elephants for their ivory tusks.

2. VIRUNGA NATIONAL PARK

Africa's oldest national park, Virunga is famous for its rare mountain gorillas. It is also home to many other animals such as 700 bird species, and 20,000 hippos. Sadly, over 175 rangers have been killed here protecting these animals.

3. OKAPI WILDLIFE RESERVE

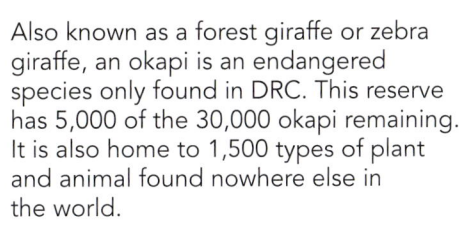

Also known as a forest giraffe or zebra giraffe, an okapi is an endangered species only found in DRC. This reserve has 5,000 of the 30,000 okapi remaining. It is also home to 1,500 types of plant and animal found nowhere else in the world.

4. SALONGA NATIONAL PARK

A tropical rainforest reserve along the Congo River, the park is home to 40 per cent of the world's bonobos, a small primate similar to a chimpanzee. Bush elephants, Congo peacocks and crocodiles also live in the area. Thanks to their efforts, Salonga has now been removed from UNESCO's Danger List.

DEMOCRATIC REPUBLIC OF THE CONGO

5. KAHUZI-BIEGA NATIONAL PARK

The park is known for its population of rare eastern lowland gorillas, which has halved since the 1990s. There are now only 8,000 left. Many people live on the edges of the park, so there are problems with hunting and illegal mining.

CONGO CONSERVATIONISTS

The population of mountain gorillas is actually recovering despite all DRC's problems, through the actions of park rangers and conservationists. UNESCO has supported them, working with the Congolese government and wildlife NGOs, such as the World Wildlife Fund (WWF). But the situation is still very difficult. A lack of security makes it hard for conservationists to visit the area safely. Thanks to their bravery, and that of the park rangers, endangered species are still being protected.

REBUILDING AFTER WAR

CHAPTER 7 : IN TIMES OF CRISIS: HUMAN CONFLICT

The impact of conflict on World Heritage sites may be felt long after the fighting has ended. As order returns, governments focus on rebuilding infrastructure such as roads, schools and hospitals. However, the reconstruction of heritage is seen as important, too, as it contributes to a country's identity.

The symbolic status of heritage sites also makes the process of restoration political. Debates on how best to rebuild a site can become very heated. UNESCO tries to find a way through all these and work with the different groups involved to ensure the best outcome for the heritage site.

People are killed during wars and many things are destroyed or damaged, but international law recognises that some actions in war are actually crimes, bringing about unnecessary death, damage or suffering. UNESCO has worked for deliberate destruction of cultural heritage to be treated as a war crime. In 2016, in the first case of its kind at the International Criminal Court (ICC) in The Hague, Netherlands, a rebel from Mali was found guilty of war crimes for destroying cultural heritage in Timbuktu.

OLD BRIDGE OF MOSTAR

The historic city of Mostar, in Bosnia and Herzegovina, is most famous for its beautiful 16th-century Old Bridge across the Neretva River. Bosnia was part of former Yugoslavia and was involved in the 1990s wars that saw this country break apart. In 1993, Mostar was shelled, and the Old Bridge collapsed.

Once peace was agreed in Bosnia, UNESCO helped organise the rebuilding of the bridge as well as the restoration of historic houses nearby. As far as possible, the same materials and building techniques were used to rebuild the bridge as per its original construction. In 2005, Mostar became a World Heritage site. Today, the Old Bridge is a major tourist attraction.

BAMIYAN BUDDHAS

The two giant standing Buddha statues carved into rocks at Bamiyan in Afghanistan were among the biggest statues in the world. They dated from the 3rd to 6th centuries. In 2001, during the civil war in Afghanistan, Taliban forces blew up the Buddhas. People around the world were shocked by this act of destruction.

As order has returned, it has not been easy to agree what to do about the destroyed statues – some people want to recreate them, others want to leave their places (niches) empty as a memorial. UNESCO has worked to bring together experts from around the world, local residents and the Afghan government to try to agree a way forward in line with recommendations made by the World Heritage Committee.

TIMBUKTU

Timbuktu, in Mali, on the edge of the Sahara Desert, became an important trading town and centre of Islamic learning between the 12th and 16th centuries. Its people built elaborate mud-brick mosques and mausoleums, giving it a World Heritage listing in 1988. But in 2012, during the Malian civil war, armed rebels occupied Timbuktu and damaged or destroyed many buildings. The town was placed on the World Heritage Danger List.

Once the rebels had been driven out, the government of Mali and UNESCO started a programme of reconstruction of the mausoleums, which was completed in 2015. The European Union (EU) and UNESCO gave money to help the works. However, Timbuktu remains on the Danger List because the security situation is still poor and there is a risk from heavy rains and flooding.

CHAPTER 8:
LOOKING TO

When World Heritage sites first began in 1978, few people would have guessed how successful the List would be. Countries now make great efforts to have their treasures designated by UNESCO. Currently more than 1,700 sites in 179 countries are candidates for listing.

Just applying for World Heritage status has the effect of stepping up conservation efforts at a local and national level. Better legal protection is put in place for sites and campaigns for listing usually involve local people, media and businesses.

It is not enough, though, simply to make sure a site is listed. Along with ongoing maintenance, there is a constant need to educate new generations about the value of sites and why it is important to protect them. Publicity and use of the media play an important role in this. Working with local NGOs and associations is another way of involving citizens in heritage protection.

Today, heritage is not only about individual monuments or natural wonders. Increasingly, it includes cultural traditions, journeys and whole ways of living. Heritage 'sites' run across national boundaries, and it is recognised that the international dimension of World Heritage is very important.

```
SOME BENEFITS OF WORLD
HERITAGE STATUS:
```

- It brings a higher degree of legal protection to a site against new building and other development.
- Heritage status attracts more funding both nationally and internationally.
- Experts from around the world become involved in archaeological, restoration and conservation work.
- Specialist knowledge is shared between countries.
- A site attracts more visitors and brings money and jobs to an area.
- International pressure helps encourage decisions in favour of heritage protection when there is a conflict between it and the interests of business or development.

THE FUTURE

ARCHAEOLOGICAL SITE OF DELPHI

High in the Greek mountains, the ancient temple ruins of Delphi are a living reminder of the contribution of ancient Greece to human civilisation. The ancient Greeks believed Delphi was the centre of the world and that the Oracle, a priestess found there, could predict the future. Visitors to Delphi today can approach the temples along the same paths as their ancient Greek ancestors more than 2,000 years ago.

Around the time Delphi was listed by UNESCO (in 1987), plans were made to build an aluminium plant near the site. After UNESCO expressed its concerns, the Greek government blocked the building of the factory. A few years later, another factory planned in the area was stopped to keep Delphi protected.

CHAPTER 8: LOOKING TO THE FUTURE

SUCCESS STORIES

World Heritage status has helped protect many heritage sites and endangered species. In addition, putting sites on the Danger List leads to international co-operation and funding to remove threats and restore sites. Dozens of places that were once placed on this List have now been removed from it.

COMOÉ NATIONAL PARK

- PLACED ON DANGER LIST IN 2003
- REMOVED FROM DANGER LIST IN 2017

Comoé National Park in Côte d'Ivoire is one of the largest protected areas in West Africa, home to thousands of animal species. Its mix of rainforest and savannah habitats makes it particularly rich in plant life. Civil war in the region between 2002 and 2007 forced park managers to stop working. As a result, poaching increased and thousands of animals were killed. Uncontrolled grazing by large herds of cattle also damaged the park.

Since the war, restoring park management has been a priority. New rangers have been put in place to protect its wildlife. Local people have agreed to control grazing and are involved in patrols around the park. The decline in the population of rare chimpanzees and elephants has been halted. All this has taken time, but the park is now off the Danger List. Encouraged by this success, the government of Côte d'Ivoire is developing eco-tourism to create jobs in the area to give local people more of a stake in the future preservation of the park.

- PLACED ON DANGER LIST IN 2012
- REMOVED FROM DANGER LIST IN 2019

BIRTHPLACE OF JESUS: CHURCH OF THE NATIVITY AND THE PILGRIMAGE ROUTE, BETHLEHEM

Since the 4th century CE, a Christian church has stood at the spot in Bethlehem where Jesus Christ, the founder of Christianity, is said to have been born. It is the oldest Christian church to be used continuously since it was built. Along with other parts of Bethlehem, including Manger Square, the Church of the Nativity was made a World Heritage site in 2012. But it was also placed straight on the Danger List, because of the fragile state of the building, particularly the roof. In the surrounding area, growing traffic levels and local industries led to air pollution, damaging the church and other nearby buildings. Too many tourists and rapid urban development also posed threats.

Over seven years great efforts were made to restore the church, including repairing the roof and ancient mosaics. Meanwhile, a plan to build a tunnel under Manger Square was stopped, and new planning controls introduced to cover the centre of Bethlehem. Countries around the world gave money to pay for the restoration works. There is still a lot of work to be done in Bethlehem – in particular, it is hard to balance tourism, which is the main industry of the town, with protecting heritage. But enough progress has been made for UNESCO to remove the site from the Danger List.

CHAPTER 8: LOOKING TO THE FUTURE

CULTURAL JOURNEYS

People's culture is created over time by many influences, and heritage is often a product of a mix of cultures. This is partly because people travel, trade and explore. The routes people take are often older than the settlements they pass through – indeed many towns and cities have grown up because of them. The World Heritage Centre is now recognising some of these traditional routes.

CAMINO DE SANTIAGO

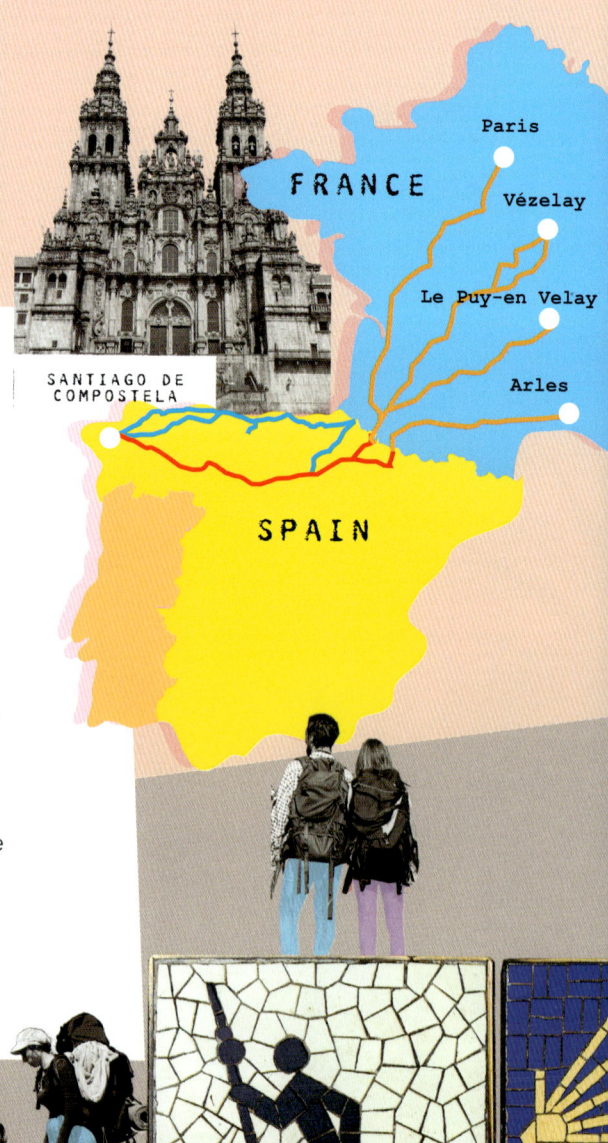

SANTIAGO DE COMPOSTELA

The magnificent cathedral of Santiago of Compostela in Spain is built over the shrine and burial place of Saint James (Santiago), an important early teacher of Christianity. Since the 9th century, pilgrims have walked the Way of St James, or Camino de Santiago, to visit the cathedral to demonstrate their faith. Nearly 1,000 years later this spiritual journey continues on foot, by bicycle or even on horseback.

There are dozens of different variations on the route, which can take months to complete. Most pilgrims start their walk in southern France, crossing the Pyrenees Mountains and then northern Spain. Today, some 1,500 kilometres of routes are today included in this World Heritage site.

The places along the route are full of the heritage of pilgrimage, from beautiful churches to medieval hostels. Because of the great length of the route, there will always be threats of development, such as new roads, housing or dams. The route also needs to be protected from large numbers of visitors, despite the benefits they bring. World Heritage status has helped greatly increase the number of pilgrims: over 300,000 of them now make this journey every year.

THE SILK ROADS

For thousands of years trade routes have been in existence between China and Europe, linking many countries and civilisations via the mountains and steppes of Central Asia. Starting in the time of the Roman Empire, trading caravans bought silk and spices from Asia to Europe, returning with wool, glassware, gold and silver. Routes also connected to the Arabian Peninsula and India.

Few people actually travelled the full length of the route, but each trade exchange in the markets along the way was an opportunity to share ideas. Cities, palaces and fortresses grew up along the Silk Roads, many of them reflecting the influences of the other cultures they traded with. The wealth created by this two-way trading helped many countries in both East and West to prosper.

Since 1990, UNESCO has been working to raise awareness of the Silk Roads and connecting routes and protect the heritage along them. This is an immense task, because the route is one of the longest human journeys on our planet, running for thousands of kilometres. Part of the route in China, Kazakhstan and Kyrgyzstan, the Tian-Shan Corridor Network, is now a cross-border World Heritage site. Other parts of the route in Iran and India have candidate status to become listed. The Silk Roads project aims to encourage sustainable tourism in these areas, some of which are remote and unspoiled landscapes.

CHAPTER 8: LOOKING TO THE FUTURE

HERITAGE EVOLUTION

To build on the success of World Heritage sites, UNESCO is thinking more broadly about what contributes towards our global culture. Just as it has done by listing trade and pilgrim routes, UNESCO wants to recognise that heritage is reflected in more than an individual building or clearly defined areas of natural beauty. Today, the idea of 'heritage' runs much wider.

Heritage definitions today include 'cultural landscapes'. These combine areas of geography, such as cities or mountains, with ways of living – Rio de Janeiro in Brazil is one example (see page 22).

Separately from World Heritage sites, UNESCO has introduced the Intangible Heritage List, that includes culture, such as traditional music, dances, processions, carnivals, sports, art and cooking. This List ranges from the reggae music of Jamaica to the making of traditional coffee in Turkey.

There is also a trend to recognise more recent heritage, such as industrial buildings from the 20th century, to protect it in a time of very rapid change. In cities today, even very modern buildings are replaced with new ones after a few years.

People today talk of 'globalisation' – the process by which business and other organisations work across and beyond national boundaries. UNESCO recognises this as true for culture, too. For example, the work of a great architect can be seen in buildings in several countries. Our world heritage is something to be shared and celebrated, now and in the future.

South Africa

KHOMANI CULTURAL LANDSCAPE

The home of the Khomani people, this site covers a vast area of the Kalahari Desert in South Africa. The Khomani are one of the last indigenous peoples of Africa still following a traditional lifestyle. The Khomani's way of life and their language are dying out, and it is hoped that the UNESCO listing will help protect their unique culture and knowledge of desert plants and animals.

VAN NELLEFABRIEK, ROTTERDAM

Built in the 1920s, this industrial complex near Rotterdam in the Netherlands was a food-processing factory until 1996. Described as a 'poem in steel and glass' it is a fine example of modern 'constructivist' architecture, giving its workers plenty of natural light. Today the building is used for offices.

LE CORBUSIER'S ARCHITECTURE

In the 20th century, Le Corbusier (1887–1965) pioneered new forms of architecture that are still influential today. This World Heritage site includes 17 of his surviving buildings in seven countries – Argentina, Belgium, France, Germany, India, Japan and Switzerland. Le Corbusier's buildings include a church (shown here), museums, offices, private houses and a public housing block. Managing a site like this is complicated, with different countries and different heritage laws in place.

GLOSSARY

apprentice – a young person who is working for someone to learn a particular skill or trade, usually for a fixed period of time

aqueduct – a structure for carrying water above ground, usually in the form of a bridge with arches

archaeology – the study of past cultures and history by digging into the ground to find the remains and traces of buildings and objects

armed conflict – fighting involving weapons between countries or between groups of people within them. Armed conflict can include wars, civil wars, uprisings and terrorism

Art Deco – a style of art, design and architecture popular in the 1920s and 1930s, using bold, geometric patterns and shapes as well as strong bright colours

artifact – an object made by humans, usually having cultural or historical value

Baroque – a style of music, art and architecture popular in Europe and Latin America in the 17th and early 18th centuries, including elaborate decorations on and within buildings

biodiversity – the variety of plant and animal life on Earth, which makes for a healthy and balanced environment

Buddhist – relating to Buddhism, a world religion founded in India in the 6th century BCE. The majority of its followers are found in Asia.

buffer zones – neutral areas of land designed to separate two elements, for example two different types of land use or two opposing groups in a war

Byzantine – art, architecture, religion and culture associated with the Byzantine or Eastern Roman Empire which lasted from the 5th to the 15th centuries in south-eastern Europe and the eastern Mediterranean

canyon – a deep, usually narrow valley with steep sides made of rock, often with a stream or river flowing through the bottom of it

caravan – in the past, a group of people and animals travelling together, often for reasons of trade, in desert areas of North Africa and Asia

caravanserai – in the past, a roadside inn in desert areas of North Africa and Asia where travellers could stop for the night

Christian – relating to Christianity, a world religion dating from the 1st century CE based on the teachings of Jesus Christ

citadel – in history, a castle or fortified part of a city, usually on high ground, where people could shelter if the city was attacked

colonists – people from one country settling in or occupying an area of another, less powerful country

conservation – saving and protecting the environment or historical buildings and objects (such as works of art or books)

ecosystem – the plants and animals living together in an area and their relationship to the physical environment

eco-tourism – tourism that tries to reduce the damage caused to the environment from people travelling, often involving holidays in areas of natural beauty

emblem – a symbol or object that stands for something else, for example the dove as a symbol of peace

endangered – in the natural world, a species of plant or animal that is under threat or at risk of dying out altogether

erosion – the gradual wearing away of soil or rock by the action of wind, rain, rivers or the sea

evolution – a process of gradual change in living things over many generations as they adapt to changes in their environment

extinct – when a plant or an animal species has died out completely and no longer exists

frescos – pictures painted on walls while the plaster is still wet

geyser – a natural spring that throws hot water and steam into the air through a hole in the Earth's surface

glaciation – the process by which land is covered by glaciers (slow-moving rivers of ice formed from snow)

habitat – the environment or place in which a plant or an animal normally lives

hammam – a public bathhouse with steam baths, sometimes known as a Turkish bath

heritage – the history, culture, traditions, buildings and objects belonging to a society, and handed on from generation to generation

Hindu – relating to Hinduism, a world religion that originated in India several thousand years ago

indigenous – people who were the first inhabitants of a country or area, as opposed to other people who arrived from elsewhere to settle there

infrastructure – the basic facilities needed for a country to operate, such as roads, power plants, water supplies and communication networks

inheritance – money, property or possessions that are received from someone who has died or which are passed on from previous generations

irrigation – watering farmland by artificial means (such as channels or pipes) so that crops will grow

Islamic – relating to the world religion of Islam, dating from the 7th century CE, practised by Muslims who follow the teachings of the Prophet Muhammad

lagoons – lakes of salt water separated from the sea by a narrow area of rock or sand

logging – the business of cutting down trees in order to use their wood for fuel or manufacturing

looting – stealing in a situation of war, conflict, rioting or similar violence

manuscripts – books or documents written by hand (not printed)

mausoleum – a building containing the dead body of a rich or famous person

medieval – a period of European history running roughly from 500 to 1500 CE, also known as the Middle Ages

megacity – a very large city with a population of over 10 million

merchants – people buying and selling goods in large quantities, often involving international trade

minaret – a tall tower attached to a mosque, from which the call to prayer is given to Muslims

mineral resources – substances found naturally in the ground that can be mined or drilled for industrial use, for example oil, gas, gold, silver, diamonds, copper and iron ore

Modernist – a style of art, design and architecture popular in the early to mid-20th century, using the latest techniques and materials instead of traditional methods

monument – a statue or building put up in memory of an important person or event; or an important historical building which is usually preserved

Neoclassical – art and architecture based on the classical designs of ancient Greece and ancient Rome, created mainly in the 18th and 19th centuries

Neolithic – the final part of the Stone Age, lasting roughly between 10000 and 3000 BCE

oasis – a small area in the middle of a desert where water and trees can be found

Ottoman – relating to the former Turkish empire in parts of Asia, Africa and Europe which lasted from the 14th century until the early 20th century

Outstanding Universal Value – the term used by UNESCO to describe something of cultural or natural significance that is so exceptional that it is important to preserve for future generations of all humanity

pilgrim – a person who travels to a holy place or shrine for religious reasons

pilgrimage – a journey undertaken for religious reasons, usually to a holy place, often long and sometimes difficult

poaching – hunting animals, birds or fish without permission or illegally

primate – a group of mammal species having hands, feet and larger brains, including apes, monkeys and humans

rainforests – thick woodland in areas of the world with very high rainfall

restoration – the act of returning something to its original condition by cleaning, repairing or reconstructing it

Roman – relating ancient Rome or to the Roman Empire, which occupied large parts of Europe, North Africa and the Middle East between 27 BCE and 476 CE

sanctuary – a place where birds or other animals can live and be protected

savannah – an area of flat open grassland, usually in Africa

shrine – a place of religious worship, usually associated with a holy individual such as a saint

species – a group of plants or animals having the same characteristics and who are able to have young with each other

spiritual – connected with thoughts and beliefs, including religious beliefs

steppes – vast treeless plains found in Russia, Ukraine and Central Asia

stonemason – a skilled worker who cuts and prepares stone for building

sustainability – ways of living, working or building that do not cause long-term damage to the environment and the Earth's resources

UNESCO – United Nations Educational Scientific and Cultural Organisation, an agency of the United Nations working to build peace through international co-operation in education, the sciences and culture

urbanisation – the building of towns and cities on land that was once countryside or used for farming

INDEX

Afghanistan *51*

Amazon *27, 48*

animals *4, 8, 15, 26–27, 28, 29, 36, 48–49, 54, 58*

Argentina *59*

archaeologists *15, 52*

architects *13, 14, 15, 16, 58, 59*

armed conflict *10, 11, 44, 45, 46, 47, 48*

Australia *37, 43*

Austria *10, 21, 29*

Belgium *9, 59*

biodiversity *9, 15, 23, 25, 27, 42, 43*

Bolivia *28*

Bosnia and Herzegovina *50*

Brazil *22, 26, 27, 58*

business *14, 24–29, 52, 58*

Cambodia *35*

Canada *8, 16, 17, 21*

charities *4, 13*

China *21, 30, 34, 57*

churches *8, 9, 13 23, 55, 56, 59*

cities *4, 7, 8, 9, 10, 13, 14, 16, 18–23, 27, 28, 31, 32–33, 35, 41, 42, 44, 46, 47, 50, 56, 57, 58*

climate change *10, 11, 25, 27, 38, 42–43*

Colombia *27*

congestion *23, 32*

construction *9, 10, 17, 19, 22, 41, 50*

Costa Rica *42*

Côte d'Ivoire *54*

Croatia *33, 44*

cultural heritage *4, 5, 6, 10, 11, 42, 50*

Czech Republic *29, 33*

Democratic Republic of the Congo (DRC) *10, 48–49*

deserts *4, 29, 47, 51, 57, 58*

earthquakes *11, 38, 39, 40–41*

ecology *15, 23*

economy *19, 25, 45*

Ecuador *8, 26, 27*

Egypt *6, 45*

environment *14, 115, 16, 24, 25, 27, 28, 29, 31*

Eritrea *16*

Ethiopia *9*

farming *24, 25, 26–27, 43*

fires *17, 38, 40–41*

First Nations *16*

fishing *24, 25, 26–27, 43*

floods *6, 7, 38, 40–41, 42, 51*

forests *4, 24, 25, 29, 49*

France *7, 56, 59*

Germany *9, 19, 59*

Greece *4, 53*

historians *15*

housing *22, 31, 56, 59*

India *18, 57, 59*

indigenous peoples *13, 16, 27, 58*

Indonesia *11, 36*

industry *24–29, 55*

Inuit *16*

Iran *41, 57*

Iraq *44*

Italy *7, 31, 41*

Japan *40, 59*

journeys *46, 52, 56–57*

Kazakhstan *57*

Kyrgyzstan *57*

Libya *11*

logging *10, 11, 27, 28–29*

Mali *50, 51*

Mexico *26*

mining *9, 10, 24, 25, 27, 28–29, 49*

monuments *4, 6, 9, 11, 23, 31, 32, 34–35, 52*

mountains *5, 9, 22, 28, 29, 35, 42, 48, 49, 53, 56, 57, 58*

national parks , *8, 9, 13, 16, 23, 28, 36, 37, 48–49, 54*

natural scientists *15, 23*

Nepal *5*

Netherlands *32, 50, 59*

NGOs *13, 27, 39, 49, 52*

Oman *29*

Peru *27, 35*

planners *14, 16, 20, 21, 22*

plants *4, 36, 49, 54, 58*

poaching *10, 11, 15, 48, 54*

Poland *9, 29*

pollution *10, 14, 19, 22, 23, 25, 28, 31, 32, 34, 36, 43, 55*

population *6, 18, 22, 23, 25, 26, 31, 44*

ports *20, 33, 43*

rainforests *10, 11, 25, 26, 27, 42, 44, 48–49, 54*

rangers *15, 37, 48, 49, 54*

rebuilding *39, 40, 41, 50–51*

reserves *8, 13, 26, 29, 49*

restoration *11, 14, 15, 17, 33, 39, 41, 50, 52, 55*

restorers *14, 15, 41*

roads *11, 19, 21, 27, 31, 32, 35, 50, 56*

Romans *23, 46, 47, 57*

Russia *25*

Senegal *9*

South Africa *58*

Spain *56*

Suriname *27*

Switzerland *59*

Syria *11, 44, 46–47*

terrorism *44, 45*

tourism *14, 15, 19, 21, 22, 25, 30–37, 43, 45, 50, 54, 55, 57*

travel *9, 15, 30, 32, 56, 57*

Turkey *23, 58*

Uganda *17*

United Kingdom (UK) *6, 20, 35*

United Nations *4, 39, 41*

USA *8, 10, 23, 28, 36*

Uzbekistan *21*

volunteers *13, 16, 36, 41*

war crimes *50*

wildlife *15, 28, 31, 36, 49, 54*

wildlife ranger *(see ranger)*

INDEX OF WORLD HERITAGE SITES

This index lists all the World Heritage sites featured in the book. Some names have been shortened so they can be easily found.

A

Aachen Cathedral 9

Abu Simbel 6

Acropolis, Athens 4

Aleppo, Ancient City of 11, 47

Amsterdam, 17th Century Canal Ring 32

Ancient Thebes with its Necropolis 45

Angkor 35

L'Anse aux Meadows National Historic Site 8

Arabian Oryx Sanctuary 29

Asmara 16

B

Bam 39, 41

Bamiyan Valley 51

Bethlehem, Birthplace of Jesus 55

Bosra, Ancient City of 46

Buganda Kings, tombs at Kasubi 17

C

Camino de Santiago 56

Carpathians, Ancient Beech Forests 29

Comoé National Park 54

Crac des Chevaliers and Qal'at Salah El-Din 46

D

Damascus, Ancient City of 46

Delphi 53

Dresden, Elbe Valley 19

Dubrovnik, Old City of 33, 44

E

Edinburgh, Old and New Towns 13

El Vizcaino Whale Sanctuary of 26

Everglades National Park 10, 23

F

Florence, Historic Centre of 41

G

Galápagos Islands 8, 26

Garamba National Park 48

Gorée, Island of 9

Great Barrier Reef 43

Great Wall (China) 34

Guanacaste Conservation Area 42

I

Istanbul, Historic Areas of 23

J

Jaipur City 18

K

Kahuzi-Biega National Park 49

Khomani Cultural Landscape 21

Komodo National Park 36

Krakow, Historic Centre of 9

L

Lake Baikal 25

Lalibela, Rock-Hewn Churches 9

Le Corbusier, Architectural Work of 59

Liverpool, Maritime Mercantile City 20

M

Machu Picchu, Historic Sanctuary 35

Mesa Verde National Park 8

Mostar, Old Bridge Area 50

N

Nahanni National Park 8

Northern Syria, Ancient Villages of 47

O

Okapi Wildlife Reserve 49

P

Palmyra 44, 47

Potosi 28

Prague, Historic Centre of 33

Q

Quebec, Historic District of 21

Quito 8

R

Rio de Janeiro, Carioca Landscapes 22, 58

Royal Salt Mines (Poland) 9

S

Sagarmatha National Park 5

Salonga National Park 49

Samarkand 21

SGang Gwaay 17

Shuri-Jo, Gusuku Sites 40

Silk Roads 46, 57

Simien National Park 9

Statue of Liberty 38

Stonehenge, Avebury and Associated Sites 35

Sumatra, Tropical Rainforest 11

T

Timbuktu 50, 51

U

Uluru-Kata Tjuta National Park 37

V

Van Nellefabriek 59

Venice and its Lagoon 6, 7, 31, 41

Vienna, Historic Centre of 10, 21

Virunga National Park 48

Y

Yellowstone National Park 8, 28

Yosemite National Park 36

FURTHER INFORMATION

WEBSITES

UNESCO

UNESCO World Heritage Centre

whc.unesco.org/en

The starting point for information about World Heritage sites, including the history of World Heritage, details about how listings work and the latest news about saving our heritage worldwide. Each of the 1,154 World Heritage sites has its own page with photographs, descriptions and maps. There are sections covering themes such as climate change and tourism.

UNESCO Intangible Cultural Heritage

ich.unesco.org/en

This site explains what Intangible Cultural Heritage is, with detailed information about all 584 cultural traditions listed by UNESCO. It is run separately from the World Heritage sites and is governed by its own convention.

INFORMATION SOURCES AND DISCLAIMER

Statistical information in this book has been taken as far as possible from the websites and publications of UNESCO and other United Nations agencies, or from official websites of World Heritage sites.

The information given is as up-to-date as possible at the time of printing this book. However, the on-going management of the World Heritage List and historic events means that some of facts and figures are liable to change.

GENERAL

African Parks

www.africanparks.org

A non-profit organisation which runs 19 national parks in 11 African countries, several of which are listed by UNESCO. Full of information about wildlife protection.

Edinburgh World Heritage

ewh.org.uk

This well-presented site explains how heritage conservation works in practice in Scotland's historic capital city.

National Geographic UNESCO page

www.nationalgeographic.com/travel/world-heritage

Beautiful photographs, videos and travel articles featuring some of the best UNESCO-listed heritage sites from around the world.

National Parks Service, USA

www.nps.gov/index.htm

Most of the USA's 24 World Heritage sites are in national parks. Find out more at the US National Park Service website.

BOOKS

The World's Heritage: The Definitive Guide to all 1073 World Heritage Sites

HarperCollins and UNESCO publications, 5th edition
A comprehensive guidebook covering all World Heritage sites.

Parks Canada

www.pc.gc.ca/en/pn-np

The website of Canada's National Parks, several of which have UNESCO listed status.

Venice In Peril

www.veniceinperil.org

This charity has worked for 50 years to restore the cultural heritage of Venice, Italy. The site has fascinating details about conservation projects to protect monuments and works of art.

World Heritage UK

worldheritageuk.org

A UK organisation that focuses on and promotes the work of the UK World Heritage sites.

Many of the World Heritage sites mentioned in this book will have their own websites where you can find more information.